"Our Way of Proceeding"

William A. Barry, S.J.

"OUR WAY OF PROCEEDING"

*To Make the Constitutions
of the Society of Jesus
and Their Complementary Norms Our Own*

THE INSTITUTE OF JESUIT SOURCES
Saint Louis

Number 19 in Series 4: Studies in Jesuit Topics

Published by

The Institute of Jesuit Sources
3700 West Pine Boulevard
Saint Louis, MO 63108
 tel: [314] 977-7257
fax: [314] 977-7263

Library of Congress Catalogue Card Number 97-73844
ISBN 1-880810-30-1

To My Fellow Jesuits

CONTENTS

INTRODUCTION TO THE DOCUMENTS

This workbook takes for granted that each user has a copy of *The Constitutions of the Society of Jesus and Their Complementary Norms* promulgated by the Thirty-fourth General Congregation.[1] In this introduction I want to say something about the way this book is constructed.

The Thirty-fourth General Congregation decided to keep the *Constitutions* as Ignatius wrote them and as they were approved by the First General Congregation, but to indicate in the text those parts that had been abrogated, modified, or explained by successive congregations. The congregation also approved *Complementary Norms* taken from previous congregations, but especially from the latest congregations, which modify or explain the *Constitutions*. Any future edition of the *Constitutions* has to include these *Norms*. In the English edition published in the United States, these are printed on the pages opposite the corresponding section of the *Constitutions*.

The book called *Constitutions of the Society of Jesus* includes five documents from the time of Ignatius.[2] The *Formula of the Institute of the Society of Jesus* comes in two parts, the bull *Regimini militantis Ecclesiæ* of Sept. 27, 1540, in which Paul III established the Society, and the bull *Exposcit debitum* of July 21, 1550, in which Julius III reconfirmed that establishment. The centerpiece of each of these two bulls is the *Five Paragraphs (Quinque capitula)* of the founders of the Society, setting out their vision of the Society of Jesus. In our edition of the *Constitutions,* these five paragraphs are printed side by side so that we can see how experience dictated some changes. Since the *Formula* is approved expressly by these two popes, it is considered the Society's "fundamental inspiration and code, comparable to St. Benedict's Rule for Monks." "Olivier Mannaerts, one of Ignatius' contemporaries, also reveals the attitude of the early Jesuits regarding *Regimini* and *Exposcit:* 'Those two

---

[1] John W. Padberg, S.J., ed. (Saint Louis: Institute of Jesuit Sources, 1996).

[2] St. Ignatius of Loyola, *The Constitutions of the Society of Jesus,* trans. with introduction and commentary by George E. Ganss, S.J. (St. Louis: Institute of Jesuit Sources, 1970), 45.

bulls of the Apostolic See contain, as in a treasure house, the whole essence of our way of life, that essence which other orders call the Rule.'"³

The *Formula* is followed by *The General Examen and Its Declarations,* two documents intended for postulants who want to enter the Society. Then come the final two documents emanating from the time of Ignatius, *The Constitutions of the Society of Jesus* and their *Declarations.* Both the *General Examen* and the *Constitutions* were originally written separately from their *Declarations.* Since the time of Francis Borgia, the *Declarations* for both the *General Examen* and the *Constitutions* have not been printed separately in most editions, but are inserted below the passages they explained. They are traditionally printed in italics as well.

The latest edition of the *Constitutions* published by the Institute of Jesuit Sources includes the translation of George Ganss and the new translation of the *Complementary Norms* approved by GC 34. The *Complementary Norms* are printed on the page facing the page in the *Constitutions* to which they are complementary.

That edition of the text, which each Jesuit of the United States Assistancy has already received, has a longer and more detailed explanation of the origin of the texts and of the meaning of the symbols. I have only intended to give a short summary here to orient the user of this present book.

My purpose is to set out a process by which individual Jesuits and groups of Jesuits might appropriate the spirit and spirituality of the text we have been given by our latest congregation. As Father General Kolvenbach states in his preface to this edition,

> Most gladly, then, my dearest brothers, do I now present to you our renewed Constitutions and their Complementary Norms, to be considered in your personal and communal prayer and to be observed in the spirit in which they have been written. Thus, with the help of God, may these, as Master Ignatius proposed, be "a certain path to him" in our enthusiastic following out of our mission in the Church, as "servants of the mission of Christ" under the leadership of the Roman Pontiff for the greater praise and glory of Christ and for the good, the salvation, and the consolation of our fellow men and women, to whom we are sent in any region of the world whatsoever. (no. 8)

My hope is that the method I present will be a help for us to deepen our grasp of our "certain way to him." Throughout this process our underlying desire ("id quod volo") will be **to have such an interior knowledge of our way of proceeding that we will almost instinctively act in this way.** For example, we will instinctively turn first to God for help in any situation before any deliberation or discussion or action because we have imbibed so deeply Ignatius's conviction as stated in Part X of the Constitutions: "The Society was not instituted by human means; and neither is it through them that it can be

---

³ Ibid.

INTRODUCTION

preserved and developed, but through the omnipotent hand of Christ, God and our Lord" [812].

I propose to select sections from the *Constitutions* and *Norms* for individual prayer and reflection. So that a person need not carry two books around for such prayer and reflection, this book will contain all texts suggested for prayer and reflection. I have divided each week into six days, and propose matter for each of those days. My hope is that most Jesuits who use this book will also gather in small groups each week to discuss the fruit of their prayer. The Constitutions are our way to God, not "my" way; the more we can talk with one another about our understanding and appropriation of "our way," the more deeply will we come to be the kind of "friends in the Lord" that Ignatius and the first companions envisaged. Our apostolic community life will be greatly enhanced by conversations on "our way to him." Moreover, we will be able more comfortably and naturally to find words with which to share our spirituality with colleagues, students, and others if we have found some ease in expressing our deepest experience with each other.

The Society of Jesus can only be true to itself if each of its members and all of us together have imbibed the spirituality that animated Ignatius and the first companions. At the end of his study of Ignatius and the founding of the Society, André Ravier writes as follows:

Ignatius founded the Society of Jesus only because he first, and several companions with him, Favre, Laynez, Xavier, Borgia, etc., had, at the call of Christ and through his grace, "wished to love more and to distinguish themselves in the total service of this eternal King and universal Lord," Jesus Christ. In founding a religious order on this framework, Ignatius was taking a fearful risk: the Society of Jesus, at each moment of its history, would be worth no more than were the companions. Would they give to the call of the "king of the Kingdom" the response which Ignatius and his authentic sons would give? Everything depends on that: upon fidelity of each companion, at each minute, in each place, depends the fidelity of the *corpus Societatis* to its vocation in the Church "to the service of God our Lord," and for the greater glory of God the Father.[4]

The Society of Jesus is ourselves; its vitality depends on us and on how we follow "our way to God."

Preliminary Observations

As we enter upon this journey of prayer and reflection, let us recall Ignatius's observations on prayer. As we begin each period of prayer, Ignatius suggests

---

[4] André Ravier, *Ignatius of Loyola and the Founding of the Society of Jesus* (San Francisco: Ignatius Press, 1987), 478.

that we take a moment or even longer to recall that we are in the presence of God and to make an appropriate gesture of recognition of that fact.

> A step or two away from the place where I will make my contemplation or meditation, I will stand for the length of an Our Father. I will raise my mind and think how God our Lord is looking at me, and other such thoughts. Then I will make an act of reverence or humility. (*Sp.Ex.*, no. 75)

Notice that the perspective is from God to the one praying; it is God's initiative from the start. The focus is taken off me. God is contemplating me. Also the body is asked to pray. Finally, notice the great importance Ignatius places on reverence. Further, he suggests that we make a preparatory prayer asking "that all my intentions, actions, and operations may be ordered purely to the service and praise of the Divine Majesty." Finally, the most important of the preludes to prayer is to ask for "what I want." During these weeks of prayer and reflection on the Constitutions, let us keep in mind the underlying desire just mentioned, namely, **to have such an interior knowledge of our way of proceeding that we will almost instinctively act in this way.** For each day I will suggest a more specific desire, but it may not be amiss to say now that this underlying desire could be consciously expressed before each prayer period. Finally, it would be good after each period of prayer to take a few moments to note down what happened during the period, moments of consolation or desolation, of excitement or languor, and so forth. Not only will such notes be of help in the repetitions at the end of each week, but they will also be helpful for the group meetings when we try to talk together about what we are learning about our way of proceeding.

Note that references such as [50] indicate one or more paragraphs of the *Constitutions.* References such as no. 50 indicate one or more paragraphs of the *Complementary Norms.* Unless otherwise noted, any page numbers refer to the edition of the *Constitutions and Norms* described above. In a few instances, there are references to other documents, such as the *Spiritual Exercises.* Such references and texts are clearly indicated at the appropriate place.

In order to make a clear distinction between the texts of the *Constitutions* and those of the *Norms,* the former are set in a serifed typeface, those of the latter in sans serif (like the last seven words and the rest of this Introduction).

WEEK I, DAY 1

This text not only speaks to the Society's continuing need to recognize its nature and mission and to renew itself through its general congregations, but also speaks to us, its members. This norm gives the rationale for the kind of process we are undertaking with the use of this book. The Society's nature and charism arise from the graces experienced during the Spiritual Exercises by Ignatius and the first companions and their subsequent conversations and deliberations. The Formulas of 1540 and 1550 name the first companions. They were human beings like ourselves with names and personal histories who as young men experienced God's call.

Preparation for Prayer: see p. 3 of this volume.

What do I desire? That I may experience the founding moments of my own vocation to the Society, especially through the Spiritual Exercises.

Preamble to the Complementary Norms

1   The Society of Jesus intends always to take a very close look at its own nature and mission, in order that, faithful to its own vocation, it can renew itself and adapt its life and its activities to the exigencies of the Church and the needs of the men and women of our times, according to its proper character and charism.

2   §1. The character and charism of the Society of Jesus arise from the Spiritual Exercises which our holy father Ignatius and his companions went through. Led by this experience, they formed an apostolic group rooted in charity, in which, after they had taken the vows of chastity and poverty and had been raised to the priesthood, they offered themselves as a holocaust to God, so that serving as soldiers of God beneath the banner of the cross and serving the Lord alone and the Church his spouse under the Roman Pontiff, the vicar of Christ on earth, they would be sent into the entire world for "the defense and propagation of the faith and for the progress of souls in Christian life and doctrine."

§2. The distinguishing mark of our Society, then, is that it is at one and the same time a companionship that is religious, apostolic, sacerdotal, and bound to the Roman Pontiff by a special bond of love and service.

I ask the Lord to help me to recall some of the key moments of the Exercises (over the years) that have been significant for my life as a Jesuit; for instance, times when I recognized with deep feeling that I was a loved sinner; when I felt freed of an inordinate attachment or addiction that hindered my response to the Lord's call; times when I felt the desire to know, love, and follow Jesus and was convinced that he wanted me as his companion; times when I desired or desired to desire to be so like Jesus that I would be treated as he was treated (third degree of humility).

I ask the Lord to help me recall times when I felt the companionship of others, especially fellow Jesuits; times when I felt the confirmation of my own sense of being called by Jesuit superiors or Church authorities. Savor these moments. These are the founding experiences of the Society as it continues its history of service in the Church.

WEEK I, DAY 2

God, who needs no one, no thing, has created us and calls us to this Institute as our pathway to God. And our way is through ministry, and a broad notion of ministry at that.

Preparation for Prayer: see p. 3 of this volume.

What do I desire? That I may experience the founding moments of my own vocation to the Society.

Formula of the Institute of **Julius III**

1   Whoever desires to serve as a soldier of God beneath the banner of the cross in our Society, which we desire to be designated by the name of Jesus, and to serve the Lord alone and the Church, his spouse, under the Roman Pontiff, the vicar of Christ on earth, should, after a solemn vow of perpetual chastity, poverty, and obedience, keep what follows in mind. He is a

member of a Society founded chiefly for this purpose: to strive especially for the defense and propagation of the faith and for the progress of souls in Christian life and doctrine, by means of public preaching, lectures, and any other ministration whatsoever of the word of God, and further by means of the Spiritual Exercises, the education of children and unlettered persons in Christianity, and the spiritual consolation of Christ's faithful through hearing confessions and administering the other sacraments. Moreover, he should show himself ready to reconcile the estranged, compassionately assist and serve those who are in prisons or hospitals, and indeed to perform any other works of charity, according to what will seem expedient for the glory of God and the common good. Furthermore, he should carry out all these works altogether free of charge and without accepting any salary for the labor expended in all the aforementioned activities. Still further, let any such person take care, as long as he lives, first of all to keep before his eyes God and then the nature of this Institute, which is, so to speak, a pathway to God; and then let him strive with all his effort to achieve this end set before him by God, each one, however, according to the grace which the Holy Spirit has given to him and according to the particular grade of his own vocation.

For Prayer, Reflection, and Discussion

I ask God to help me recall times when I kept my eyes on God. What were those times like? Would I want to experience such times again? I ask God to help me recall times when I found our Institute to be a pathway to God. In what concrete ways? As I read the purposes of our founding, what strikes me? What resonates positively? What negatively?

WEEK I, DAY 3

The last four general congregations, reflecting on the Society's mission in the light of the Formula *and the* Constitutions *and of the circumstances of today's world, have definitively interpreted for today's Society our Institute, our pathway to God. We ask God to help us to know how we have been affected by the events since Vatican II and by the work of these four congregations.*

Remember that we are asking for God's revealing light, a grace not in our power. We have gone through a turbulent period since Vatican II, a period of light and of darkness; hence, we may experience light and darkness in our prayer now.

Preparation for Prayer: see p. 3 of this volume.

What do I desire? That I may have an interior knowledge of how God's hand has been in the work of the four congregations since Vatican II.

Preamble to the Complementary Norms

4   §1. According to these documents, explained by later general congregations, the mission of the Society consists in this, that as servants of Christ's universal mission in the Church and in the world of today, we may procure that integral salvation in Jesus Christ which is begun in this life and will be brought to its fulfillment in the life to come. Therefore the mission of the Society today is defined as the service of faith, of which the promotion of justice is an absolute requirement.

§2. The service of faith and the promotion of justice constitute one and the same mission of the Society. They cannot, therefore, be separated one from the other in our purpose, our action, our life; nor can they be considered simply as one ministry among others, but rather as that ministry whereby all our ministries are brought together in a unified whole.

§3. This mission also includes, as integral dimensions of evangelization, the inculturated proclamation of the Gospel and dialogue with members of other religions. Hence, in our mission, the faith that seeks justice is a faith that inseparably engages other traditions in dialogue and evangelizes cultures.

5   §1. These Complementary Norms of the Constitutions of the Society of Jesus, for the most part taken principally from decrees of general congregations, try to gather together the principal fruits of today's renewal as a present-day expression of the genuine image of the Society and as a necessary help in applying its Constitutions according to their deeper requirements.

§2. But if this genuine image of the Society cannot be perfectly converted into normative expressions, these Norms must always be referred back to this image as expressed in the *Formula of the Institute* and in the Constitutions. For this image is the primary pattern, whose outline the present Norms ought to express by their very nature, and in whose light they must be interpreted.

I let the memories of the times since Vatican II rise to the surface, trusting that the Spirit will bring to consciousness what I need to remember. If I entered the Society before Vatican II, what contrasts do I remember? What gains? What losses? What are my emotional reactions to the documents I am now reading and to my memories?

WEEK I, DAY 4

Here we ponder the raison d'être for the fourth vow and the question whether the Holy Spirit has given us the grace to carry out this vocation.

Preparation for Prayer: see p. 3 of this volume.

What do I desire? That I may have an interior knowledge of the nature of our vocation, the kind of knowledge that impelled Ignatius and the first companions to take the extraordinary step of asking permission to put the Society and each Jesuit under special vow to accept any mission from the pope.

Formula of the Institute of Paul III

3   All the members should know not only when they first make their profession but daily, as long as they live, that this entire Society and each one individually are campaigning for God under faithful obedience to His Holiness [the pope] and the other Roman Pontiffs who will succeed him. And although the Gospel teaches us, we know from orthodox faith, and we firmly profess that all the faithful in Christ are subject to the Roman Pontiff as to their head and the vicar of Jesus Christ, still, for the greater humility of our Society and the perfect mortification of each one of us and the abnegation of our own wills, we have judged that it is of the greatest profit to us to go beyond the ordinary obligations and bind ourselves by a special vow, so that whatever the present Roman Pontiff and others to come will wish to command us with regard to the progress of souls and the propagation of the faith, or wherever he may be pleased to send us to any regions whatsoever, we will obey at once, without subterfuge or excuse, as far as in us lies. We pledge to do this whether

he sends us among the Turks or to other infidels, even to the land they call India, or to any heretics or schismatics, or to any of the faithful.

4   Therefore, those who will come to us should, before they take this burden upon their shoulders, ponder long and seriously, as the Lord has counseled, whether they possess among their resources enough spiritual capital to complete this tower; that is, whether the Holy Spirit who moves them is offering them so much grace that with his aid they have hope of bearing the weight of this vocation. Then, after they have enlisted through the inspiration of the Lord in this militia of Christ, they ought to be prompt in carrying out this obligation which is so great, being clad for battle day and night [Eph. 6:14; 1 Peter 1:13].

For Prayer, Reflection, and Discussion

How does this vow strike me in our present circumstances? What positive and negative resonances does it set off in me? What is God revealing to me through these movements, both for me and for us?

How am I affected by these questions: Is the Holy Spirit offering me so much grace that with his aid I have hope of bearing this vocation? Is the Holy Spirit offering **us** (for example, my group, my community, my province, the present Society) so much grace that with his grace we have hope of bearing this vocation?

What else does God raise to our consciousness as we let these texts touch us?

WEEK I, DAY 5

The training of our own men necessitated a shift from the norm for professed houses. Thus by 1550 the difference between professed houses and colleges was foreseen. We will see in Part VI that recent congregations have definitively interpreted our poverty, removing the distinction between professed houses and nonprofessed houses. The decision not to recite the Divine Office in common and not to have a distinctive habit and monastic way of life was a radical departure for a religious order. It was made because of the purpose for which the Society was founded, namely, the good of souls. We have become so accustomed to our way of life that we may forget the religious reason why the first companions sought it and fought for it. Because Jesuits are expected to find God in their ministry and to discipline their hearts and minds and bodies for this way of finding God, the Society could ask for these departures from traditional practices.

Preparation for Prayer: see p. 3 of this volume.

What do I desire? That I may have a profound interior knowledge of the reasons given for the vow of poverty and of how I and my brothers can live out this vow today.

Formula of the Institute of Julius III

7   From experience we have learned that a life removed as far as possible from all infection of avarice and as like as possible to evangelical poverty is more gratifying, more undefiled, and more suitable for the edification of our neighbors. We likewise know that our Lord Jesus Christ will supply to his servants who are seeking only the kingdom of God what is necessary for food and clothing. Therefore our members, one and all, should vow perpetual poverty in such a manner that neither the professed, either as individuals or in common, nor any house or church of theirs can acquire any civil right to any annually recurring produce, fixed revenues, or possessions or to the retention of any stable goods (except those which are proper for their own use and habitation); but they should instead be content with whatever is given them out of charity for the necessities of life.

8   However, since the houses which the Lord will provide are to be dedicated to labor in his vineyard and not to the pursuit of scholastic studies; and since, on the other hand, it appears altogether proper that workers should be provided for that same vineyard from among the young men who are inclined to piety and capable of applying themselves to learning, in order that they may be a kind of seminary for the Society, including the professed Society; consequently, to provide facilities for studies, the professed Society should be capable of having colleges of scholastics wherever benefactors will be moved by their devotion to build and endow them. We now petition that as soon as these colleges will have been built and endowed (but not from resources which it pertains to the Holy See to apply), they may be established through authorization from the Holy See or considered to be so established. These colleges should be capable of having fixed revenues, annuities, or possessions which are to be applied to the uses and needs of the students. The general or the Society retains the full government or superintendency over the aforementioned colleges and students; and this pertains to the choice of the rectors or governors and of the scholastics; the admission, dismissal, reception, and exclusion of the same; the enactment of statutes; the arrangement, instruction, edifica-

tion, and correction of the scholastics; the manner of supplying them with food, clothing, and all the other necessary materials; and every other kind of government, control, and care. All this should be managed in such a way that neither may the students be able to abuse the aforementioned goods nor may the professed Society be able to convert them to its own uses, but may use them to provide for the needs of the scholastics. These students, moreover, should have such intellectual ability and moral character as to give solid hope that they will be suitable for the Society's functions after their studies are completed, and that thus at length, after their progress in spirit and learning has become manifest and after sufficient testing, they can be admitted into our Society. Since all the members should be priests, they should be obliged to recite the Divine Office according to the ordinary rite of the Church, but privately and not in common or in choir. Also, in what pertains to food, clothing, and other external things, they will follow the common and approved usage of reputable priests, so that if anything is subtracted in this regard in accordance with each one's need or desire of spiritual progress, it may be offered, as will be fitting, out of devotion and not obligation, as a reasonable service of the body to God.

For Prayer, Reflection, and Discussion

What are my reactions to these texts? Is evangelical poverty more gratifying (joyful) for me? Do I have experiences of joy in poverty? Do I trust that the Lord will provide what is necessary? Note, too, that Ignatius wanted any penances and mortifications to be matters of personal devotion, not obligation, done in accord with discerning love. How do these ideas strike me?

WEEK I, DAY 6

Preparation for Prayer: see p. 3 of this volume.

What do I desire? That I may have a deep knowledge and love of our way to God.

Formula of the Institute of **Julius III**

9   These are the matters which we were able to explain about our profession in a kind of sketch, through the good pleasure of our previously mentioned sovereign pontiff Paul and of the Apostolic See. We have now done this, that we may give succinct information, both to those who ask us about our plan of life and also to those who will later follow us if, God willing, we shall ever have imitators along this path. By experience we have learned that the path has many and great difficulties connected with it. Consequently we have judged it opportune to decree that no one should be permitted to pronounce his profession in this Society unless his life and doctrine have been probed by long and exacting tests (as will be explained in the Constitutions). For in all truth this Institute requires men who are thoroughly humble and prudent in Christ as well as conspicuous in the integrity of Christian life and learning. Moreover, some persons will be admitted to become coadjutors either for spiritual or temporal concerns or to become scholastics. After sufficient probations and the time specified in the Constitutions, these too should, for their greater devotion and merit, pronounce their vows. But their vows will not be solemn (except in the case of some who with permission from the superior general will be able to make three solemn vows of this kind because of their devotion and personal worth). Instead, they will be vows by which these persons are bound as long as the superior general thinks that they should be retained in the Society, as will be explained more fully in the Constitutions. But these coadjutors and scholastics too should be admitted into this militia of Jesus Christ only after they have been diligently examined and found suitable for that same end of the Society. And may Christ deign to be favorable to these our tender beginnings, to the glory of God the Father, to whom alone be glory and honor forever. Amen.

Recapitulation of the Week

Go back over the points that struck you most forcefully, either positively or negatively, this week. Ask the Lord to help you to know and love at a deep level what it means to be a companion of Jesus today.

In preparation for meeting with one's group reflect on what your experiences might be saying to us as a group of Jesuits. The first companions, after their experience of making the Exercises in Paris, were delighted to discover that they had received a common call. They discovered this by talking with one another about their experience of the Exercises. Gradually they discovered that God had a vocation for them as a group. As we talk to one another, we hope to discover what God wants to reveal to **us** as a group, what God is calling **us** to at this significant time in the history of the Society and of the Church.

WEEK II, DAY 1

The Examen *was intended by Ignatius for postulants, so that they might get a quick overview of the Society which they felt called to join. Here we have the first words they would read about the purpose of the Society and of its name.*

Preparation for Prayer: see p. 3 of this volume.

What do I desire? That I may have a profound appreciation of and gratitude for being called to the company of Jesus.

General Examen

[1]   This least congregation, which at its earliest foundation was named the Society of Jesus by the Holy See, was first approved by Pope Paul III, of happy memory, in the year 1540. Later it was confirmed by the same Holy Father in 1543 and by his successor Julius III in 1550. On other occasions too it is mentioned in different briefs and apostolic letters granting it various favors, after highly approving and confirming it.

[3]   2. The end of this Society is to devote itself with God's grace not only to the salvation and perfection of the members' own souls, but also with that same grace to labor strenuously in giving aid toward the salvation and perfection of the souls of their neighbors.

[7]   5. In addition to the three vows mentioned, the professed Society also makes an explicit vow to the present or future sovereign pontiff as the vicar of Christ our Lord. This is a vow to go anywhere His Holiness will order, whether

among the faithful or the infidels, without pleading an excuse and without requesting any expenses for the journey, for the sake of matters pertaining to the worship of God and the good of the Christian religion.

For Prayer, Reflection, and Discussion

Have I had experiences that resonate with Ignatius's desire that his congregation be known as the Company of Jesus? Do I recall my reactions to these words when I first paid attention to them? What are my reactions to the vow of obedience to the Roman Pontiff? I ask the Lord to show me his dream for the Society and for me and us.

I also ask the Lord to help me recall instances when I experienced God in carrying out my principal ministry. The end of the Society means that we find God in our ministry.

WEEK II, DAY 2

Ignatius was convinced that God wants the Society to exist and that God alone can keep it in existence. In addition, Ignatius believed that exterior laws alone will not preserve the Society, but that the interior law of charity and love can do so. The process upon which we are now engaged as we use this book begs the Holy Spirit to fan the flame of such charity and love in me and in all of us.

Preparation for Prayer: see p. 3 of this volume.

What do I desire? That I may have a deep interior knowledge and conviction that God still wants to keep the Society in existence.

Preamble to the Constitutions

[134]   Although God our Creator and Lord is the one who in his Supreme Wisdom and Goodness must preserve, direct, and carry forward in his divine service this least Society of Jesus, just as he deigned to begin it; and although on our own part what helps most toward this end must be, more than any exterior constitution, the interior law of charity and love which the Holy Spirit

writes and imprints upon hearts; nevertheless, since the gentle disposition of Divine Providence requires cooperation from his creatures, and since too the vicar of Christ our Lord has ordered this, and since the examples given by the saints and reason itself teach us so in our Lord, we think it necessary that constitutions should be written to aid us to proceed better, in conformity with our Institute, along the path of divine service on which we have entered.

[136]   The purpose of the Constitutions is to aid the body of the Society as a whole and its individual members toward their preservation and increase for the divine glory and the good of the universal Church.

For Prayer, Reflection, and Discussion

The purpose of the Constitutions is "to aid us to proceed better . . . along the path of divine service," "to aid the body of the Society as a whole and also its individual members." They are our pathway to God. I ask for the grace to keep God and our pathway to God before my eyes always; I ask the same grace for the Society as a whole; I ask for a profound grasp of this pathway, to be able to see each part as a step in the pathway to God.

It has been said that the *Autobiography,* the *Spiritual Exercises,* and the Constitutions all issue from Ignatius's mystical experience in Manresa, especially the experience on the banks of the Cardoner. These three documents are "three ways of communicating the same experience" (Joseph Veale, "From Exercises to Constitutions: A Spirit in Search of a Body," in *The Constitutions of the Society of Jesus: Incorporation of a Spirit* [Rome: Secretariat of Ignatian Spirituality, 1993], 7). The Constitutions are for us Jesuits the way Ignatius tried to communicate to his companions the way to God shown to him in his experience at Manresa.

WEEK II, DAY 3

By choosing the order of execution, Ignatius shows that he prefers experience, the concrete and personal. The spiritual and apostolic health of the whole body depends on the spiritual and apostolic health of each member. Ignatius takes step-by-step the building up of the body through formation of the individual members. He describes a process of formation and growth into which the individual enters, is formed in spirit and in learning and is then incorporated. The steps follow the first five parts of the Constitutions:

- *Welcome (Part I)*
- *Separation in consolation (Part II)*
- *Forming in spirit and in virtue (Part III)*
- *Learning and pastoral apprenticeship (Part IV)*
- *Incorporation, becoming members of the body (Part V)*

This shape, this literary form, is the key to understanding properly each part and paragraph and sentence in the texts (see Veale, "From Exercises to Constitutions," 7).

Preparation for Prayer: see p. 3 of this volume.

What do I desire? That I may have a deep interior grasp of the process of growth that Ignatius thought to be important.

Preamble to the Constitutions

[135]   Moreover, while the consideration which comes first and has more weight in the order of our intention regards the body of the Society as a whole, whose unity, good government, and preservation in well-being for the greater divine glory are primarily in view, nevertheless, inasmuch as this body is made up of its members, and what occurs first in the order of execution pertains to the individual members, in regard to their admission, progress, and distribution into the vineyard of Christ our Lord, it is from this consideration that we shall begin, with the help which the Eternal Light will deign to communicate to us for his own honor and praise.

WEEK II, DAY 4

God has a project in creation, the Kingdom of God. Everything else is secondary to God's project; hence, the Ignatian principles of tantum-quantum *and indifference. Ignatius and his first companions came to believe that the founding of the Society of Jesus is part of God's project, a means to the end God intends. In other words, God's project envisioned not only the call of each of them as individuals to serve Christ, but also the creation of an unbreakable bond between them in a congregation, a body animated by the Spirit of Jesus. It is not just a question of God's dream for me, but of God's dream for us and for those who will follow us in the Society. There is a danger in trying to institutionalize a charism; the charism is lost without the spirit. Therefore we make this exercise, so that the spirit may animate our lives as Jesuits.*

Preparation for Prayer: see p. 3 of this volume.

What do I desire? That I may have a deep interior knowledge and love of God's project and of the place of the present Society and of myself in this project.

The Principle and Foundation and the Constitutions

Human beings are created to praise, reverence, and serve God our Lord, and by means of doing this to save their souls. The other things on the face of the earth are created for human beings, to help them in the pursuit of the end for which they are created. From this it follows that we ought to use these things to the extent that they help us toward our end, and free ourselves from them to the extent that they hinder us from it. To attain this it is necessary to make ourselves indifferent to all created things, in regard to everything which is left to our free will and is not forbidden. Consequently, on our own part we ought not to seek health rather than sickness, wealth rather than poverty, honor rather than dishonor, a long life rather than a short one, and so on in all other matters. Rather, we ought to desire and choose only that which is more conducive to the end for which we are created (*Sp.Ex.,* no. 23).

For Prayer, Reflection, and Discussion

I let myself recall times of great excitement about God's project and my call to be a part of it. Spend some time savoring those times and talking with Jesus about them.

WEEK II, DAY 5

*In Paris the first companions made the Spiritual Exercises under Ignatius (and after Ignatius left, under Pierre Favre). Each of them came to the belief that he was called to follow Jesus under his standard of poverty, humiliation, and humility and to serve him in the Holy Land. Each was overjoyed to find out that the others had the same call. In 1539 in Rome during the First Deliberation they discovered that God had a call for **them** as a group, to form the Company of Jesus. Thus, as a result of their conversations with one another, they moved from a conviction that God had a project "for me" to a conviction that God had a project "for us." The Institute was the way of spelling out that project "for us."*

Preparation for Prayer: see p. 3 of this volume.

What do I desire? That I may have a deep interior knowledge that I am called to follow Jesus, that I have been given the desire to serve Jesus under his standard.

The Call of the King and the Following of Christ under His Standard

If we give consideration to such a call from the temporal king to his subjects, how much more worthy of our consideration it is to gaze upon Christ our Lord, the eternal King, and all the world assembled before him. He calls to them all, and to each person in particular he says: "My will is to conquer the whole world and all my enemies, and thus to enter into the glory of my Father. Therefore, whoever wishes to come with me must labor with me, so that through following me in the pain he or she may follow me also in the glory" (*Sp.Ex.*, no. 95).

For Prayer, Reflection, and Discussion

I ask the Lord to help me to recall experiences of realizing that God had a project for me, and times when I realized that he had a project for us, that I was part of a group of men called by God to serve together.

WEEK II, DAY 6

Preparation for Prayer: see p. 3 of this volume.

What do I desire? That I may have a deep interior knowledge that I am called to follow Jesus, that I have been given the desire to serve Jesus under his standard.

WEEK III, DAY 1

The choice of candidates is tied to the end of the Society, "the divine service." Ignatius presumed that God wants the Society to exist; hence, that God is calling men to its ranks. But the provincial has to try to discern the call; he cannot just depend on a man's own sense of call. A healthy interplay between the discernment of an individual and its confirmation or disconfirmation by the discernment of competent authority is presumed in these texts.

Preparation for Prayer: see p. 3 of this volume.

What do I desire? That I may have a profound interior knowledge and love of "our way of proceeding," especially of God's desires for our Society today.

The Choice of Candidates for the Society

Constitutions, Part I

[142]   3. It is highly important for the divine service to make a proper selection of those who are admitted and to take care to know their abilities and vocation well. Therefore if the one who has the aforementioned authority does not do all of that by himself, he should have, among those who reside more permanently in the same place as himself, someone to aid him in getting to know, conversing with, and examining those who come. This helper should possess discretion and skill in dealing with persons so different in temperament and disposition, so that things may be carried out with greater clarity and satisfaction on both sides for the divine glory.

[143]   4. Both the one who has the authority to admit and his helper ought to know the Society well and be zealous for its good functioning, so that no other consideration will be able to deter him from what he judges in our Lord to be more suitable for his divine service in this Society. Therefore he should

be very moderate in his desire to admit *[C]*. Furthermore, so that he may be more free from disordered affection where occasion for it might exist (as in the case of relatives or friends), anyone in whom this danger is in any way feared ought not to perform the function of examiner.

[144]   *C. Just as care should be taken to cooperate with the divine motion and vocation, endeavoring to secure in the Society an increase of workers for the holy vineyard of Christ our Lord, so also much thought should be given so as to admit only those who possess the qualifications required for this Institute, for the divine glory.*

[147]   1. To speak in general of those who should be admitted, the greater the number of natural and infused gifts someone has from God our Lord which are useful for what the Society aims at in his divine service, and the more assurance the Society has about these gifts, the more suitable will the candidate be to be admitted.

[152]   4. In view of the end of our Institute and our manner of proceeding, we are convinced in our Lord that to admit persons who are very difficult or unserviceable to the congregation is not conducive to his greater service and praise, even though their admission would be useful to themselves.

[161]   13. The extrinsic gifts of nobility, wealth, reputation, and the like, just as they do not suffice if those others are lacking, so they are not necessary when the others are present. But to the extent that they aid toward edification, they render more apt to be admitted those who would be fit without them because they have the other qualifications mentioned above. The more an applicant is distinguished for those qualifications, the more suitable will he be for this Society unto the glory of God our Lord, and the less he is distinguished by them, the less suitable. But the measure to be observed in all things will be taught by holy unction of the Divine Wisdom [1 John 2:20, 27] to those who are charged with this matter, undertaken for his greater service and praise.

[163]   1. Although the charity and zeal for souls practiced by this Society in accord with the end of its Institute embraces persons of every kind to serve them and help them in the Lord of all to attain to beatitude, nevertheless, when there is a question of incorporating persons into the same Society, that charity and zeal ought to embrace only those who are judged useful for the end it seeks (as has been said [143, 144]).

The Choice of Candidates for the Society
Complementary Norms, Part I

25 §1. In order to attain the goals of probation, sufficient human maturity and suitable preparation are requirements for candidates.

§2. For this purpose, candidates can in different ways be recommended to certain selected fathers and brothers who will help them towards obtaining maturity in their vocation while they prepare for entrance into the novitiate by means of studies and apostolic experiments.

26 §1. A personal examination should be accurately made of candidates' lives, endowments, and aptitude for the Society, their right intention, their defects of both soul and body, as well as of any impediments or hindrances that may happen to exist, paying special attention to and adapting to our own times the instructions found in the *Examen* and the Constitutions.

§2. Other appropriate means should also be used so that the Society knows them fully; therefore, unless the candidates are already well known, information should be sought concerning their health, virtues, education, practice of the Christian life, temperament, talents, studies completed and with what success, the condition of their family and its social circumstances; and, when necessary for a fuller knowledge of them, a recommendation should be sought from those skilled in psychology. The secrecy of consultation, the candidate's freedom, and norms established by the Church are, however, to be strictly safeguarded.

For Prayer, Reflection, and Discussion

As I read these texts, I ask the Lord to enlighten me on the nature of our calling as Jesuits. What reactions do I have to these passages? Do I sense the danger of elitism in the criteria? Are there safeguards against the spirit of elitism? How do I feel about the criteria for entrance? Do I have any personal reactions, for example, about my own qualifications? about my own judgments about candidates? Do I encourage vocations to the Society now? Do I believe that God still calls men of our culture to our Society? What can I (we) do to help young men to hear God's call to our Society?

WEEK III, DAY 2

Here Ignatius gives the Society directives on how to receive those who have been accepted for first probation. Once again we see the emphasis on trying by all means, but especially by prayer, to discover if there is, in fact, a call from God to enter the Society for life.

Preparation for Prayer: see p. 3 of this volume.

What do I desire? That I may have a profound interior appreciation of the seriousness of our vocation and of our cooperation with the grace of God.

The First Probation (Postulancy)

Constitutions, Part I

[190]   1. We are strongly convinced in our Lord that it is of great importance for the service of his Divine and Supreme Majesty through this least Society that those received in it not only be tested for a long time before incorporation into it but also be well known before they are admitted to the probation which is made by living in common with those of the house. Hence, it is good that next to where we live in common there be quarters where those being admitted may stay as guests for twelve to twenty days, or longer if it seems good to the superior, so that during this time they may be more fully informed about the Society and the Society may become better acquainted with them in our Lord.

[192]   2. Admission to this house, called the house of the first probation, may be given more quickly to applicants who clearly appear to be apt to serve God our Lord in this Society. On the other hand, those who are clearly seen to be unsuitable may, with the assistance of advice and whatever other means charity may dictate so that they may serve God our Lord elsewhere, be dismissed right away.

[193]   3. Sometimes the clarity needed on the Society's side may still be lacking even after the candidate has expressed his desire, been tactfully questioned about the first category of impediments, and had the substance of our Institute and the trials and difficulties entailed in it explained to him. If this should happen, even though the applicant manifests an efficacious determination to enter the Society to live and die in it (and in general no one lacking such a determination should be admitted to the first probation), the final reply and decision should be put off for a time, during which the case can be considered and commended to God our Lord and appropriate means can be employed to get to know the applicant and also to test his steadfastness. But the extent of this postponement and investigation should be left to the prudent consideration of the one having authority to admit; and he should always keep in view the greater service of God.

[197]   4. After the decision has been made in our Lord that it is proper to admit such an applicant to probation, he may enter, dressed as he customarily was or in the manner in which each one finds more devotion, unless the superior thinks otherwise. He should be placed as a guest in the aforementioned house or separate quarters, and on the second day he should be told how he should conduct himself in that place, and especially that (unless the superior for urgent reasons thinks otherwise) he should not deal either by word of mouth or by writing with others from outside or inside the house, except for certain persons who will be assigned to him by the superior. The purpose is that he may with greater freedom deliberate with himself and with God our Lord about his vocation and intention to serve his Divine and Supreme Majesty in this Society.

For Prayer, Reflection, and Discussion

We note how often Ignatius refers to God's action toward the Society and to the Society's purpose of serving the Lord; also how Ignatius expects that decisions will be "made in the Lord." What are my reactions to these texts? What do they say about the Society and about the Society's way of proceeding? What comes to mind with regard to how we should proceed in the modern world?

WEEK III, DAY 3

In these passages Ignatius indicates how the Society should proceed with regard to those who should be dismissed. Note the insistence on discernment, on kindness and charity, on justice, on the desire to keep the goodwill of those who leave. Yet at the same time the one in authority and his helpers have to keep uppermost in mind the good of the Church and of the Society.

Preparation for Prayer: see p. 3 of this volume.

What do I desire? That I may have a profound knowledge and love of our way of proceeding with regard to men who enter and leave.

On Dismissal of Those Who Have Entered the Society
Constitutions, Part II

[204]   1. Just as it is useful for the end sought in this Society, namely, the service of God our Lord by helping souls, to preserve and multiply the workers who are found apt and useful for carrying this work forward, so is it also expedient to dismiss those who are found unsuitable, and who as time passes make it evident that this is not their vocation or that their remaining in the Society does not serve the universal good. However, just as there should not be excessive readiness in admitting candidates, so should there be even less to dismiss them; instead, one should proceed with much consideration and pondering in our Lord. And although the more fully one has been incorporated into the Society, the more serious ought the reasons to be, nevertheless, no matter how advanced the incorporation may be, there may be situations when a given person can and ought to be separated from the Society, as will be seen in chapter 2.

[209]   1. The discreet charity of the superior who has the authority to dismiss ought to ponder before God our Lord the causes which suffice for dismissal. But to speak in general, they seem to be of four kinds.

[210]   2. The first cause is present if it is perceived in our Lord that someone's remaining in this Society would be contrary to the honor and glory of God, because this person is judged to be incorrigible in some passions or vices which offend his Divine Majesty. The more serious and culpable these are, the less ought they to be tolerated, even if they might not scandalize others because they are occult.

[212]   3. The second cause is present if it is perceived in the Lord that to retain someone would be contrary to the good of the Society. Since this is a universal good, it ought to be preferred to the good of a single individual by one who is sincerely seeking the divine service. This would be the case if in the course of the probation impediments or notable defects should be discovered which the applicant failed to mention earlier during the examination, or if experience should show that he would be quite useless and a hindrance rather than a help to the Society because of his notable incompetency for any task whatever; much more so if it is judged that he would be harmful by the bad example of his life, especially if he shows himself unruly or scandalous in words or deeds. To tolerate this would be attributable not to charity but to its very opposite on the part of one who is obliged to preserve the peace and well-being of the Society which is in his charge.

[216]   4. The third cause is present if someone's remaining is seen to be simultaneously against the good of the Society and of the individual. For example, this could arise from the body, if during the probation such illnesses and weakness are observed in a person that it seems in our Lord that he would be unable to carry on the labor which is required in our manner of proceeding

in order to serve God our Lord in that way. It could also arise from the temper of his mind, if the one who was admitted to probation is unable to bring himself to live under obedience and to adapt himself to the Society's manner of proceeding, because he is unable or unwilling to submit his own judgment, or because he has other hindrances arising from nature or habits.

[218]   1. With those who must be dismissed, that manner ought to be employed which before God our Lord is likely to give greater satisfaction to the one who dismisses as well as to the one dismissed and to the others within and without the house. For the satisfaction of the one who dismisses, for the causes mentioned above, three points should be observed.

[220]   2. The first point to be observed is that he should pray and order prayers in the house for this intention (although the person's identity remains unknown), that God our Lord may make his holy will known in this case.

[221]   3. The next point is that he should confer with one or more persons in the house who seem more suitable and hear their opinions.

[222]   4. The third point is that, ridding himself of all affection and keeping before his eyes the greater divine glory and the common good, and the good of the individual as far as possible, he should weigh the reasons on both sides and make his decision to dismiss or not.

[223]   5. For the satisfaction of the one dismissed, three further points ought to be observed. One, pertaining to the exterior, is that as far as possible he should leave the house without shame or dishonor and take with him whatever belongs to him.

[225]   6. The second point, pertaining to the interior, is to try to send him away with as much love and charity for the house and as much consoled in our Lord as is possible.

[226]   7. The last, pertaining to his personal condition, is to try to guide him in taking up some other good means of serving God, in religious life or outside it as may seem more conformable to his divine will, assisting him with advice and prayers and whatever in charity may seem best.

[227]   8. Likewise, for the satisfaction of the others inside and outside the house, three things ought to be observed. One is that everything possible should be done to ensure that no one is left troubled in spirit by the dismissal; satisfactory grounds for it can be given to whoever needs it, touching as little as possible upon faults in the person which are not public (even if he has them).

[229]   9. A second is that they should not be left disaffected or with a bad opinion in his regard, as far as this is possible. Rather, they should have compassion for him and love him in Christ and recommend him in their prayers to the Divine Majesty, that God may deign to guide him and have mercy on him.

What are my own attitudes toward and feelings about men who have left, especially friends? How do I react to these texts and to the attitudes they hope for in us? Do I have any misgivings about how the Society has treated men who have left? Do I have any lingering resentments about those who have left? What do I need from the Lord? From my brothers in Christ?

WEEK III, DAY 4

The purpose of the novitiate is to enable novices "to make progress, both in spirit and in virtues along the path of divine service." Ignatius draws on his practical advice in the Spiritual Exercises to help novices develop their spiritual life. Note how the Complementary Norms (CN) work with the Constitutions toward the same end, but take into account changing times. Adaptation to "persons, places, and times" is a principle of Ignatius's Constitutions. Note that CN no. 44 stresses both the formative and probationary nature of the novitiate and that CN no. 45 speaks of the apostolic end of the Society as the principle that rules all of formation. Formation is a process of integration into the apostolic body of the Society. Just as does Ignatius in the Constitutions, so too CN no. 46 stresses the experimental nature of the Jesuit novitiate.

Preparation for Prayer: see p. 3 of this volume.

What do I desire? That I may have a profound knowledge of how God desires the Society to grow and develop. To obtain this grace would be to understand and love the practical spirituality of the whole of Jesuit life, especially in its formative aspects.

The Preservation and Progress of Those Who Remain in Probation: The Novitiate

Constitutions, Part III

[243] 1. Just as with regard to the admission of those whom God our Lord calls to our Institute by giving them suitable ability for it, and the dismissal of those who through lack of such ability reveal that they have not been called by his Divine

Wisdom, there is need of the considerations expounded so far, so also due consideration and provident care must be employed toward preserving in their vocation those who are being retained and tested in the houses or colleges, and toward enabling them to make progress both in spirit and in virtues along the path of the divine service, in such a manner that care is also taken of the health and bodily strength necessary to labor in the Lord's vineyard. Consequently, what pertains to the soul will be treated first [243–91] and then what pertains to the body [292–306].

[244]   2. In regard to the soul, it is of great importance to keep those who are in probation away from all imperfections and from whatever can impede their greater spiritual progress. For this purpose it is highly expedient that they should cease from all communication by conversation and letters with persons who may dampen their resolves; further, that while they advance along the path of the spirit, they should deal only with persons and about matters which help them toward what they were seeking when they entered the Society for the service of God our Lord.

Complementary Norms, Part III

53   Although entrance into the novitiate should entail a real separation from the life previously led in the world, superiors should nevertheless provide that the novices, while consistently maintaining a spirit of recollection, should have sufficient social contact with their contemporaries (both within and outside the Society). Likewise the necessary separation from parents and friends should take place in such a way that genuine progress in affective balance and supernatural love is not impeded.

Constitutions, Part III

[250]   4. All should take special care to guard with great diligence the gates of their senses (especially the eyes, ears, and tongue) from all disorder, to preserve themselves in peace and true humility of their souls, and to show this by their silence when it should be kept and, when they must speak, by the discretion and edification of their words, the modesty of their countenance, the maturity of their walk, and all their movements, without giving any sign of impatience or pride. In all things they should try and desire to give the advantage to the others, esteeming them all in their hearts as if they were their superiors [Phil. 2:3] and showing outwardly, in an unassuming and simple religious manner, the respect and reverence appropriate to each one's state, so that by consideration of one another they may thus grow in devotion and praise God our Lord, whom each one should strive to recognize in the other as in his image.

The Formation of the Novices

Complementary Norms, Part III

44   §1. The novitiate is a time at once of formation and of probation, during which the grace of vocation should be cultivated and during which it should already manifest its fruitfulness.

§2. But for those who entered as indifferents, it is also an opportune time to discern their future vocation to brotherhood or priesthood.

45   §1. The apostolic purpose is to be considered the principle that regulates the entire formation of our members. Therefore, the whole formation of our members from the novitiate on must be understood and promoted as a process of integration into the apostolic body of the Society, as a formation in mission.

46   §1. A vocation is to be tested by various experiments that, in St. Ignatius's view, constitute the specific characteristic of the novitiate; these must place the novices in those circumstances wherein they can give evidence of what they really are and show how they have made their own the spiritual attitudes proper to our vocation. New experiments, of the sort that would fulfill this purpose today, ought to be prudently and boldly pursued.

§2. Primacy in the novices' formation should be given to the Spiritual Exercises, since of all the experiments they are the chief and fundamental one. Let them, therefore, be well prepared for, made at the most advantageous time, and presented in all their force and spiritual vigor.

47   §1. Education towards familiarity with God in prayer should be carried out in the apostolic atmosphere of the Exercises. The daily exercises of piety should tend to arouse personal love for Christ and teach the seeking of familiar communion with God in all things. Care should also be taken that the novices clearly understand how the different means presented in the Constitutions themselves (examination of conscience, prayer, meditation, reading, and so forth) serve to complement one another.

§2. Besides the time of prayer prescribed for all in probation (see no. 67, §2), novices should give themselves to prayer for another half hour daily. The length of this time of prayer can be discreetly prolonged or lessened for each one according to the judgment of the director.

49   Let self-denial be primarily exercised humbly and simply in the everyday demands of our vocation. Particular mortifications should, however, be undertaken, under the guidance of obedience, as indicated by the individual's requirements, the Church's call, and the world's needs. Moreover, let the novices learn, in theory and by practice, to shape their life by austerity and sobriety.

50   The practice of community life should both develop the brotherhood of our members and benefit the affective maturity of the novices.

51   Human virtues are to be fostered, because they make the apostolate more fruitful and religious life happier; among these virtues are goodness of heart, sincerity, strength of mind and constancy, diligent care for justice, openness of mind and respect for differing beliefs of others, politeness, and other similar qualities.

For Prayer, Reflection, and Discussion

As I (we) ponder these practical regulations, do I (we) grasp the spirit that animates them? How do I (we) react to these regulations? Do I (we) have any questions about how they are being carried out in our province and assistancy? Do these regulations speak to my (our) life style? What is God revealing to us as we ponder these texts?

WEEK III, DAY 5

The novices begin to pick up some fundamentals of the Society; for example, poverty and how Ignatius views it; obedience as trust that God would lead a person through the relationship with the superior, with the novice director (and, by extension, with other superiors) as men who are lovable; the way of correcting with love.

Preparation for Prayer: see p. 3 of this volume.

What do I desire? That I may have a profound knowledge and love of how God wants us to live our lives as Jesuits; namely, that I (we) may have a deep understanding and love of the Society's way of proceeding.

The Preservation and Progress of Those Who Remain in Probation: The Novitiate
Constitutions, Part III

[254]   7. So that they may begin to experience the virtue of holy poverty, all should be taught that they must not have the use of anything as their own. However, it is not necessary for them to dispossess themselves of their property during

the probation, except where the superior should order this, after expiration of the first year, because he judges that for some person such property is an occasion of temptation and of making less progress in spirit because of his placing some disordered love and confidence in it. In that case the disposition should be made in conformity with the counsels of Christ our Lord. However, it is left to the devotion of each one to apply his property, or a part of it, to one pious work rather than to another, according to what God our Lord will give him to perceive as being more conducive to his divine service, as was stated in the *Examen* [53–59].

Complementary Norms, Part I

32   §1. One who enters the novitiate, if he has personal property, is to promise that he will renounce it whenever after the completion of the first year of probation superiors will mandate it.

§2. This promise, which is neither a vow nor a mere intention, is made under this condition: "if he will have persevered and the superior will have ordered him."

Constitutions, Part III

[263]   12. It will be beneficial to have a faithful and competent person to instruct and teach the novices how to conduct themselves inwardly and outwardly, to encourage them to this, to remind them of it, and to give them loving admonition—a person whom all those who are in probation may love and to whom they may have recourse in their temptations and open themselves with confidence, hoping to receive from him in our Lord counsel and aid in everything. They should be advised, too, that they ought not to keep secret any temptation which they do not tell to him or to their confessor or to the superior, being happy to have their entire soul completely open to him. Moreover, they will tell him not only their defects but also their penances or mortifications, or their devotions and all their virtues, with a pure desire to be directed if in anything they have gone astray, and not wishing to be guided by their own judgment unless it is in agreement with the opinion of him whom they have in place of Christ our Lord.

[265]   13. Temptations ought to be guarded against by their opposites, for example, if someone is seen to be inclined to pride, by exercising him in lowly matters deemed helpful for humbling him; and similarly of other evil inclinations.

[269]   15. The procedure to be followed in corrections and penances will be left to the discreet charity of the superior and of those whom he may delegate in his place, who will measure them in accord with the disposition of persons and with general and individual edification, for the divine glory *[N]*. Each one ought to accept them in a good spirit with a genuine desire of his emendation and spiritual profit, even if they are not given for a defect that is blameworthy.

[270]   *N. In giving corrections it should be noted that, while discretion may change this order in a particular case, those who fall into a fault ought to be admonished the first time with love and with gentleness, the second time with love and in such a way that they feel abashed and ashamed, the third time with love and the instilling of fear. However, the penance for public faults must be public, disclosing only what will most conduce to the edification of all.*

[282]   22. It will be very specially helpful to perform with all possible devotion the tasks in which humility and charity are practiced more; and, to speak in general, the more one binds himself to God our Lord and shows himself more generous toward his Divine Majesty, the more will he find God more generous toward himself and the more disposed will he be to receive daily greater graces and spiritual gifts.

[288]   26. All should strive to keep their intention right, not only in regard to their state of life but also in all particular details, in which they should aim always at serving and pleasing the Divine Goodness for its own sake and because of the incomparable love and benefits with which he has anticipated us rather than for fear of punishments or hope of rewards, although they ought to draw help from these also. They should often be exhorted to seek God our Lord in all things, removing from themselves as far as possible love of all creatures in order to place it in the Creator of them, loving him in all creatures and all creatures in him, in conformity with his holy and divine will.

For Prayer, Reflection, and Discussion

What stands out as I ponder these texts prayerfully? What are my reactions? Do I trust the Society to take care of my (and our) material needs? To lead me (us) to God and to participation in God's project? Have I found my superiors lovable in the way Ignatius pictures the novice director? Do I feel some pricks of conscience as I ponder these texts? Do I (we) have any serious questions about the Society's faithfulness to the spirit of these texts?

Week III, Day 6

Preparation for Prayer: see p. 3 of this volume.

What do I desire? That I may have a profound knowledge and love of how God wants us to live our lives as Jesuits; that is, that I (we) may have a deep understanding and love of the Society's way of proceeding.

Recapitulation of the Week

Go over the salient points that touched you in preparation for meeting with your group. Continue to ask God to reveal to you what is for your own and the Society's greater good.

Week IV, Day 1

Obviously, the first Jesuits did not originally intend to have colleges and universities or to accept young men who needed to be formed. Experience taught them, and rather early, both that colleges and universities would be fruitful areas for the apostolate and that they needed to accept young men so that they might carry on the work that God seemed to be calling the Society to do. One of the hallmarks of Ignatian spirituality is to pay attention to experience as a locus where we will find God's will for us. Note how the new direction taken is tied to the purposes for which the Society was founded. Note as well the way that Ignatius keeps his and our eyes on God: "with the favor of the Divine and Eternal Wisdom and for his greater glory and praise," "desiring to preserve and increase the Society for the greater glory and service of God our Lord." These words serve to remind us that we carry on this project of internalizing the spirit of the Constitutions, and indeed all our actions, at God's initiative and under his guidance.

Preparation for Prayer: see p. 3 of this volume.

What do I desire? That God give me (us) a deep knowledge and love of our way of proceeding, especially with regard to studies and learning.

The Learning and Other Means of Helping Their Neighbor That Are to Be Imparted to Those Who Are Retained in the Society

Constitutions, Part IV

PREAMBLE

[307]   1. The end steadfastly pursued by the Society is to aid its own members and their neighbors in attaining the ultimate end for which they were created. For this, in addition to the example of one's life, learning and skill in expounding it are required. Hence, once the proper foundation of abnegation of themselves and the needed progress in virtues is seen to be present in the new members, it will be necessary to provide for the edifice of learning, and of skill in employing it so as to help make God our Creator and Lord better known and served. For this, the Society undertakes colleges as well as some universities, where those who prove themselves worthy in the houses but have entered the Society unequipped with the necessary learning may be instructed therein and in the other means of helping souls *[A]*. Hence, with the favor of the Divine and Eternal Wisdom and for his greater glory and praise, we shall treat first of what pertains to the colleges and then of the universities.

[308]   *A. The aim and end of this Society is, by traveling through the various parts of the world at the order of the supreme vicar of Christ our Lord or of the superior of the Society itself, to preach, hear confessions, and use all the other means it can with the grace of God to help souls. Consequently it has seemed to us necessary, or at least highly expedient, that those who will enter the Society be persons of good life and sufficient learning for the aforementioned work. However, those who are both good and learned are relatively few; and even among these few, most are already seeking rest from their labors. We have thus found it a quite difficult matter to increase the numbers of this Society with such good and learned men, in view of the great labors and the great abnegation of self which are required in the Society. Therefore all of us, desiring to preserve and increase the Society for the greater glory and service of God our Lord, have thought it wise to take another path, that of admitting young men whose good habits of life and talent give hope that they will become both virtuous and learned in order to labor in the vineyard of Christ our Lord. We shall likewise accept colleges under the conditions stated in the apostolic bull, whether these colleges are within universities or outside of them; and, if they are within universities, whether these universities are governed by the Society or not. For we are convinced in our Lord that in this way greater service will be given to his Divine Majesty, with those who will be employed in that service ·being multiplied in number and making progress in learning and virtues.*

General Norms

59 §1. Since the formation of all our members is directed toward the apostolic objective of the Society, namely, that they may be able "with the help of God to benefit both their own souls and those of their neighbors," this objective is to be considered the principle which regulates the entire formation of our members.

§2. The choice made by General Congregation 32 concerning the mission of the Society in today's world as the service of faith, of which the promotion of justice is an absolute requirement, must give new vigor to our formation, so that it may respond to the requirements of evangelization in a world that is often infected by atheism and injustices, and may equip our members for entering into dialogue with people and meeting the cultural problems of our times.

60 We should conceive and plan for the total formation of our members as a process of progressive integration of the spiritual and community life, of the apostolate, and of studies, in such a way that the richness of the spiritual life should be the source of the apostolate, and the apostolate in turn the motive for study and for a deeper spiritual life.

For Prayer, Reflection, and Discussion

What are my reactions as I ponder these texts? How do I react to the stress on learning and training for Jesuits to serve in the vineyard? What is God saying to me (us) as we reflect prayerfully on these texts?

WEEK IV, DAY 2

St. Ignatius presumes that God will provide the Society with generous men and women who will support our works financially. The very first chapter in this part of the Constitutions takes up the virtue of gratitude toward such generous benefactors.

Preparation for Prayer: see p. 3 of this volume.

What do I desire? That God give me (us) the grace not only to trust in his providence but also to be grateful in tangible ways to God and to those whom God sends to us as benefactors.

Our Attitude toward Benefactors

Constitutions, Part IV

[309]   1. It is highly proper for us to do something on our part in return for the devotion and generosity shown toward the Society by those whom the Divine Goodness employs as his ministers to found and endow its colleges. First of all, therefore, in every college let a Mass be said in perpetuity each week for its founder and benefactors, living and dead.

[310]   2. Likewise, at the beginning of each month all the priests in the college should be obliged, in perpetuity, to celebrate one Mass for these same persons.

Each year, too, on the anniversary of the day when the possession of the college was handed over, let a solemn Mass be celebrated in it for the founder and benefactors. All the other priests dwelling there are to celebrate Mass for the same intention.

[312]   3. On that day a wax candle is to be presented to the founder, or to one of his closer relatives, or in whatever way the founder may stipulate. The candle should contain his coat of arms or emblems of his devotions, as a sign of the gratitude due in our Lord *[C]*.

[314]   *C. This candle signifies the gratitude due to the founders, not any right of patronage or any claim belonging to them or their successors against the college or its temporal goods, for none such will exist.*

[315]   4. As soon as a college is handed over to the Society, the superior general should notify the entire Society, in order that each priest may celebrate three Masses for the living founder and the benefactors, that God our Lord may sustain them by his own hand and cause them to advance in his service. When the general learns that God has taken them from this life to the other *[D]*, he should instruct the priests to celebrate three more Masses for their souls. Whenever it is stated that Masses must be celebrated by the priests, all the rest who dwell in the colleges and are not priests ought to pray for the same intention for which the priests are celebrating. For the same obligation of showing gratitude is incumbent in the Lord on them as well as on the priests.

[316]   *D. In the case of communities, which have continuous existence, these Masses will be celebrated for their deceased members, particularly for those to whom we are more indebted in our Lord.*

[317]   5. The founders and benefactors of such colleges become in a special way sharers in all the good works of those colleges and of the whole Society.

[318]   6. In general, the Society should deem itself especially obligated to them and to their dear ones, both during their lifetime and after their death. It is bound, by an obligation of charity and love, to show them whatever service it can according to our humble profession, for the divine glory.

For Prayer, Reflection, and Discussion

Perhaps reflection on these texts will bring to mind benefactors who have made my (our) study and work possible. How do I react to Ignatius's presumption that God in his goodness will provide benefactors to found the colleges? Do I have such confidence? Do I see benefactors as God's ministers in helping our works?

WEEK IV, DAY 3

In these texts we see the practicality of Jesuit spirituality. Note the regular reference to God and God's glory and good pleasure. Recall Ignatius's own experience of being distracted from studies by religious thoughts and experiences. Here is an example from his student days in Barcelona:

> *. . . he began to study with great diligence. But one thing was very much in the way: that is, when he began to memorize, . . . there came to him new insights into spiritual matters and fresh relish, to such an extent that he could not memorize, nor could he drive them away no matter how much he resisted.*
>
> *So, thinking often about this, he said to himself: "Not even when I engage in prayer and am at Mass do such vivid insights come to me." Thus, little by little, he came to realize that it was a temptation.[5]*

Ignatius found through experience that prayer itself could be a distraction from what was for the greater glory of God.

---

[5] *A Pilgrim's Testament: The Memoirs of St. Ignatius of Loyola,* trans., with introduction by Parmananda R. Divarkar (St. Louis: Institute of Jesuit Sources, 1995), 79-80.

Preparation for Prayer: see p. 3 of this volume.

What do I desire? That God give me (us) a felt knowledge of our way of proceeding with regard to prayer and study.

The Care and Welfare of the Scholastics Admitted to Studies
Constitutions, Part IV

[339]   1. For the care and welfare of those who live in the colleges, in regard to the body and external matters, what was stated in Part III [292–306] will suffice. That is, special attention should be given to their abstaining from studies at times inopportune for bodily health, to their taking sufficient sleep, and to their observance of moderation in mental labors so as to be able to keep at them longer both during their studies and later on when using what they have studied for the glory of God our Lord.

[340]   2. In regard to spiritual matters, the same procedure as is used with those received in the houses will be used with those received in the colleges as long as they are still going through probations. However, once they have satisfactorily completed them and are devoting themselves to studies, while care must be taken that they do not through fervor in study grow cool in their love of true virtues and of religious life, still they will not at that time have much place for mortifications or for long prayers and meditations. For their devoting themselves to learning, which they acquire with a pure intention of serving God and which in a certain way requires the whole person, will be not less but rather more pleasing to God our Lord during this time of study.

[342]   3. Consequently, in addition to confession and Communion every eight days *[B]* and daily Mass, they will have one hour, during which they will recite the Hours of Our Lady, examine their consciences twice each day, and add other prayers according to each one's devotion to fill out the rest of the aforesaid hour. They will do all this according to the order and judgment of their superiors, whom they oblige themselves to obey in place of Christ our Lord.

[343]   *B. To go more often than every eight days should not be allowed except for special reasons, taking more account of need than of devotion. But neither should reception be deferred beyond eight days unless there are special reasons. For such reasons, Mass could also be omitted on some day, and for some persons the period of prayer could be lengthened or shortened. This will remain wholly within the discretionary power of the superior. The specified hour will be taken, somewhat more or less, for the recitation of the Hours of Our Lady. Nevertheless in the case of the scholastics who are not obliged to recite the Divine Office, the hour can more easily be changed at times to meditations and other spiritual exercises by which the hour is filled out, especially with some who do not advance*

spiritually by one method, so that with God's grace they may be helped more by another. This is to be done with the permission or through the order of their superiors, whose duty it will always be to consider whether, for certain reasons with particular persons, something different is more expedient, in order to carry it out while keeping in view the genuine devotion of the subjects or of the founder, and also the circumstances of persons, times, and places.

Spiritual Formation (regarding times of prayer)

Complementary Norms

67 §1. Our members during the entire time of their formation should be carefully helped to grow in prayer and a sense of spiritual responsibility towards a mature interior life, in which they will know how to apply the rule of discerning love that St. Ignatius prescribed for members after the period of their formation.

§2. To foster this growth, the Society retains the practice of an hour and a half as the time for prayer, Mass, and thanksgiving. Each one should be guided by his spiritual director as he seeks that form of prayer in which he can best advance in the Lord. The judgment of superiors is normative for each.

§3. Each one should determine with his superior what time he gives to prayer and preparation for it.

For Prayer, Reflection, and Discussion

How do I react to these texts? What resonates positively? What negatively? Do I (we) sense a challenge to my (our) attitudes and actions regarding study? Is God revealing anything to us through our reactions?

WEEK IV, DAY 4

Once again we see that the Society makes choices in the light of the purposes for which God founded it; also, that the choices have to be made in the light of changing circumstances.

Preparation for Prayer: see p. 3 of this volume.

What do I desire? That God give me (us) a felt knowledge of our way of proceeding with regard to studies and formation.

The Formation of Our Men after Novitiate

Constitutions, Part IV

[351] 1. Since the end of the learning which is acquired in this Society is with God's favor to help the souls of its own members and those of their neighbors, it is by this norm that the decision will be made, both in general and in the case of individual persons, as to what subjects Ours ought to learn and how far they ought to advance in them. And since, generally speaking, help is derived from the humane letters of different languages, logic, natural and moral philosophy, metaphysics, scholastic and positive theology, and Sacred Scripture, these are the subjects which those who are sent to the colleges should study. They will devote themselves with greater diligence to the parts which are more helpful for the end mentioned above, taking into account circumstances of times, places, persons, and other such factors, as seems expedient in our Lord to him who holds the principal charge.

[355] 2. What particular studies each individual scholastic should make will likewise be left to the discretion of the superiors. Nevertheless, when someone has aptitude, the better he is grounded in the aforementioned subjects the better will it be.

Formation in Studies

Complementary Norms, Part IV

81 §1. Since the purpose of studies in the Society is apostolic, through their studies our members should acquire that breadth and excellence in learning that are required to achieve this end.

§2. The Society confirms its proper option for a profound academic formation of its future priests—theological as well as philosophical, humane, and scientific—persuaded that, presupposing the testimony of one's own life, there is no more apt way to exercise our mission.

§3. Inasmuch as brothers participate in the apostolic activity of the Society according to the gifts received from God, they should receive appropriate theological instruction and adequate formation in what concerns their work.

§4. For this reason, our members in formation should be reminded that their special mission and apostolate during the time of study is to study.

82   Our studies should foster and stimulate those very qualities that today are often choked off by our contemporary style of living and thinking: a spirit of reflection and an awareness of deeper, transcendent values.

For Prayer, Reflection, and Discussion

What are my (our) reactions to these texts? To modern formation? Do I have trust in the Society's *formatores*? Do I (we) have questions about formation that would help me (us) to carry out our own responsibilities toward younger men in the Society?

WEEK IV, DAY 5

GC 34 has given a declaration for our times of Ignatius's directions on the matter to be studied by our scholastics. We see again that we must keep our eyes on God and God's greater glory in all things, including studies. In [358] we catch Ignatius's prudence and caution regarding the doctrine taught to Ours. He himself had profited by the method and the doctrine taught at the University of Paris, especially the doctrine and method of St. Thomas Aquinas. In no. 358 Ignatius seems to presume that the Society will have to adapt its mode of studies. The Complementary Norms give us the adaptations made by the modern Society since GC 31 and culminating in GC 34. Again we see that studies are for the purposes for which the Society exists, not just for their own sakes.

Preparation for Prayer: see p. 3 of this volume.

What do I desire? That God give me (us) a felt knowledge of our way of proceeding with regard to studies and formation.

The Formation of Our Men after the Novitiate
Constitutions, Part IV

[358]   4. The doctrine which they ought to follow in each subject should be that which is safest and most approved, as also the authors who teach it. The

rectors will take care in this regard, conforming themselves to what is decided in the Society as a whole for the greater glory of God.

The Teaching to Be Imparted to Our Members

Complementary Norms, Part IV

(a declaration regarding this text)

9 §1. The purpose of our studies is to train Jesuits to proclaim and transmit the truth revealed in Christ and entrusted to the Church. Our teaching, therefore, should faithfully adhere to what "was once given to the holy men of the faith," and should be such that, accommodating itself to changing ways of speaking and thinking, and adapting itself to the diverse cultures of the whole world, it can continually revivify that faith in human hearts.

§2. Our formation must be such that a Jesuit can be one with the people to whom he is sent, capable of communicating with them. He must be able to share their convictions and values, their history, their experience and aspirations; at the same time he must be open to the convictions and values of other peoples, traditions, and cultures.

100 Jesuits ought to put their trust in the strength of divine truth and in that inner unction of the Holy Spirit which leads the Church of Christ to all truth. Therefore they should strive to join to their studies a close familiarity with God; following this secure way, they will be safe from timidity as well as from thoughtless innovation. Let them in all matters see that their knowledge is well grounded, according to the norms which the Holy See has given to the Church and to the Society.

101 Professors should bear in mind that they do not teach in their own name, but in the Church, in accordance with the mission received from the Church, and that they teach joined together in charity in the Society of Jesus. Hence, they should let themselves be guided by the mind and will of the Church, show proper respect for the teaching authority of the Church, and have regard for the building up of the faith in their students and in all the faithful. At the same time they should keep in mind those who are separated from us.

102 Both professors and scholastics should faithfully adhere to and diligently study the written word of God along with sacred tradition. Let them also have high regard for the teaching of the holy fathers and other doctors, specifically St. Thomas, and for those authors of the Society who are highly regarded in the Church.

103 §1. Professors should clearly distinguish between matters of faith to be held by all and teachings approved by the consent of theologians. Probable, new, and personal explanations are to be proposed modestly.

§2. For more secure and profitable progress in doctrine, it will be very helpful if the professors freely and sincerely communicate to their colleagues their new ideas, even before they are published. Thus, if necessary, they can be corrected by them and can perhaps also be of benefit to them.

104   If any of our professors in his teaching departs from doctrine in accord with the magisterium of the Church, superiors ought to speak with him in order to understand well both him and his thinking; and, if occasion warrants, they should admonish him. If he does not change, superiors should not hesitate even to remove him from his teaching position, if it eventually proves necessary, observing as far as possible the statutes of the institution or faculty.

105   During their course of studies, scholastics should be taught, under the direction of their professors, to read critically and use prudently the works of those authors who have greater influence on present-day cultures. Thus they should learn how to retain what is good and to correct what is unacceptable.

For Prayer, Reflection, and Discussion

How do I react to the prudence and caution of Ignatius? Do I have reactions to my own studies? How do I react to these norms? What strikes me most forcefully? What positive and negative reactions do I have to them? What is the Lord revealing to us through these norms that derive from our general congregations? Do I have questions about the studies our men undertake, questions that come from my prayer and reflection on these texts and my experience?

WEEK IV, DAY 6

This section gives us an insight into the spirituality that Ignatius hoped for in Jesuits as they engaged in studies. It is, therefore, a good way to recapitulate the prayer and reflections of this week.

Preparation for Prayer: see p. 3 of this volume.

What do I desire? That God give me (us) a felt knowledge of our way of proceeding with regard to studies and formation.

Recapitulation

Means for Their Learning Well
the Aforementioned Subjects

Constitutions, Part IV

[360] 1. In order to make good progress in these subjects, the scholastics should strive first of all to keep their souls pure and their intention in studying right, by seeking in their studies nothing except the glory of God and the good of souls. Moreover, they should frequently beg in prayer for grace to make progress in learning for the sake of this end.

[361] 2. Next, they should have a firm resolution to be genuine and earnest students, persuading themselves that while they are in the colleges they cannot do anything more pleasing to God our Lord than to study with the intention mentioned above; likewise, that even if they never have occasion to employ the matter studied, the very toil of study, duly undertaken because of charity and obedience, is itself a very meritorious work in the sight of the Divine and Supreme Majesty.

[362] 3. The impediments which distract from study should also be removed, both those arising from excessive or improperly ordered devotions and mortifications *[A]* and those springing from external cares and occupations, whether in duties inside the house *[B]* or outside it in conversations, confessions, and other activities with one's fellowmen, to the extent that these may be avoided in our Lord *[C]*. For in order that the scholastics may be able to help their neighbors better later on by what they have learned, it is wise to postpone exercises such as these, pious though they are, until after the years of study, since there will be others to attend to them in the meantime. All this should be done with a greater intention of service and the divine glory.

[363] *A. This is the general practice. But if an individual finds it necessary to apply himself to devotion and mortification, it will be left to the discretion of the one who holds the principal charge to consider how far he should go in these matters.*

[364] *B. To give aid at some hour to those who hold these burdensome duties is not improper; but to assume them permanently is more properly the work of the coadjutors, and these can be provided to lighten this burden for those who are studying.*

[365] *C. Consequently, to avoid such hindrances those not yet in holy orders would do well to put off ordination until they complete their studies. However, because of needs that may arise it is at times necessary to dispense from this. Moreover, this work of helping the neighbors could be supplied by some who have*

finished their studies or who are sent to the colleges specially for this purpose. Likewise, for the more demanding domestic offices inside the college, it will be good to have persons who are not primarily intent upon studies, such as temporal coadjutors or persons who are there for purposes of probation rather than study.

For Prayer, Reflection, and Discussion

What are my reactions to this section? What has struck me most forcefully about formation in the Society during this week? What do I want to talk about with my group?

WEEK V, DAY 1

Formation in the Society is seen as preparation for mission. Hence, it should include experiences and practices that will foster apostolic effectiveness not only of the individual Jesuit but also of the corporate body. Note that although Ignatius prized the scholastic method of St. Thomas for study, he was well aware that effective preaching could not use the same method.

Preparation for Prayer: see p. 3 of this volume.

What do I desire? That God give me (us) a profound knowledge and love of our way of proceeding, of our way to God.

The Instruction of the Scholastics in the Means of Helping Their Neighbor

Constitutions, Part IV, Chapter 8

[400] 1. In view of the objective which the Society seeks in its studies, towards their end it is good for the scholastics to begin getting accustomed to the spiritual arms they must employ in aiding their fellowmen; and this work can be begun in the colleges, even though it is more properly and extensively done in the houses.

[401] 2. First of all, those who in the judgment of the superior should be ordained are to be taught how to say Mass not only with interior understanding and devotion but also with a good exterior manner, for the edification of

those who hear the Mass. All members of the Society should as far as possible use the same ceremonies, conforming, so far as the diversity of regions permits, to the Roman usage as being more universal and embraced in a special way by the Apostolic See.

[402]   3. Similarly, they will exercise themselves in preaching and delivering [sacred] lectures in a manner suited to the edification of the people, which is different from the scholastic manner; they should strive to learn the vernacular language well, to have prepared and have ready at hand the topics most useful for this ministry, and to avail themselves of all appropriate means to perform it better and with greater fruit for souls.

[408]   5. After they themselves have experienced the Spiritual Exercises, they should get practice in giving them to others. Each one should know how to give an explanation of them and how to make use of this spiritual weapon, since it is obvious that God our Lord has made it so effective for his service.

Apostolic Formation
Complementary Norms, Part IV, Chapter 6

106   §1. The whole process of formation through its various stages from novitiate to tertianship should favor integration into the apostolic body of the Society, so that it prepares our young men to fulfill the missions and perform the ministries which the Society may wish to assign to them.

§2. Therefore, our style of life and its attendant circumstances, both personal and communitarian, ought to favor apostolic formation, so that young Jesuits can know and understand what the people among whom they live are seeking, what they suffer, and what they lack; in a particular way they should foster solidarity with the poor, so that they learn from them how they can aid them.

§3. A certain experience of living with the poor will sometimes be necessary for our young men, to help them both to overcome limitations that may perchance spring from their own social background and to strengthen their love for the poor. However, this should take place under such conditions that it will be genuine, free of illusions, and productive of a true conversion. For this purpose, contact with the poor should be extended rather than occasional, and must be accompanied by careful reflection and integrated into training in sociocultural analysis.

107   A formation that is bound up with the activities of the province or region is also especially helpful for this. Therefore, the major superior himself or others designated by him should see that our young men are directed in this in progressive stages and by means of a variety of experiences, according to the talents of each and with a view to the apostolic works of the province or region as well as of the whole Society.

108 §1. Apostolic formation of all our members ought to be carried on in a progressive fashion under the direction of a competent coordinator, who should direct our men in formation in their apostolic activities, bring them to examine the activities critically, and help them to carry them out. This apostolic formation should be an integrated part of the curriculum of studies.

§2. Apostolic activities, which are to be undertaken as a mission from superiors, should be so arranged that they lead to a deeper level of spiritual and intellectual reflection.

§3. Scholastics should be trained for different priestly ministries. Brothers, on the other hand, should be prepared to perform the works proper to their vocation, so that they fully participate in the apostolic mission of the Society in their distinctive way.

§4. All should grow accustomed to directing others in the Spiritual Exercises under the supervision of an experienced director.

For Prayer, Reflection, and Discussion

Recall that we are on a journey of discovery of our path to God under the guidance of the Holy Spirit. Our reactions to these texts will give us matter for the discernment of spirits. Which of our reactions are of God, which indicate our resistance to God and to our following the path to God which the Constitutions are for us? Paying attention to our reactions and discerning which are of God, which not, is at the heart of Ignatian spirituality.

WEEK V, DAY 2

Regency, a time of apostolic activity prior to theological studies, was an innovation in the normal course of formation for religious. Once again, we see that the Society's formation is governed by the apostolic purposes of the Society. This text gives us a chance to reflect on our own formation experiences and on the relation of the formed Society to those of its members who are in formation and are assigned to apostolic communities for regency.

Preparation for Prayer: see p. 3 of this volume.

What do I desire? That God give me (us) a profound appreciation of our pathway to God, especially of that part of our formation called regency.

Apostolic Formation, *continued*

Complementary Norms, Part IV

109   §1. Regency, whose purpose is to contribute to a fuller religious and apostolic maturity, will be made after philosophy according to the ordinary practice in the Society; but, according to the judgment of the provincial, it may be deferred up to the time immediately preceding priestly ordination, or some other appropriate experiment may be substituted for it.

§3. During the time of teaching or experiments, care is to be taken that the scholastics' spiritual lives not only do not thereby suffer damage but, on the contrary, that they derive therefrom a proper growth. Accordingly, consideration should be given to the community where they live during regency, and their superior should have special concern for their formation.

§4. But if they experience greater difficulties in prayer and work at this time, they should learn to overcome them with magnanimity and patience in the Lord.

For Prayer, Reflection, and Discussion

I ask the Lord to help me to recall the formative experiences of my own regency to appreciate how I was led toward God and toward Jesuit apostolic prayer and effectiveness through them. I also ask his help to appreciate my role and my community's role in helping men in formation to realize the fruits of this period of their formation.

WEEK V, DAY 3

The text from the Constitutions reminds us again of how formation takes its structure from the apostolic ends of the Society. Ignatius and the early Jesuits believed that members of the Society would be required to go out to many different cultures and people. It is a difficult vocation; hence, the formation had to be designed to shape men for this arduous calling. But here again we see that Ignatius keeps before our hearts and minds that the grace of God is primary. The texts from the Complementary Norms explicate for our times how the modern Society forms its men.

Preparation for Prayer: see p. 3 of this volume.

What do I desire? That God give me (us) a profound appreciation for the way God wants to form us for his purposes.

The Instruction of the Scholastics in the Means of Helping Their Neighbor, *continued*

Constitutions, Part IV, Chapter 8

[414]   8. In general, they ought to be instructed about the manner of acting proper to a member of the Society, who has to associate with so great a diversity of persons throughout such varied places. Hence they should foresee the difficulties which may arise and the opportunities which can be grasped for the greater service of God by employing this means or that. Although all this can be taught only by the unction of the Holy Spirit [1 John 2:20, 27] and by the prudence which God our Lord communicates to those who trust in his Divine Majesty, nevertheless the way can at least be opened by some suggestions which help and prepare for the effect that is to be produced by divine grace.

Apostolic Formation

Complementary Norms, Part IV

110   In the whole course of formation, especially during philosophical and theological studies, a deep and authentic involvement with the local culture should be fostered, according to regional differences, by sharing the life and experiences of those peoples among whom we work and by trying to understand their cultures from within. Yet care should also be taken to promote unity of minds and hearts in the Society, based on genuine Ignatian spirituality; and a truly universal spirit, proper to our vocation, is to be reinforced by various experiences, such as by participating in international meetings of those in formation, or by receiving part of one's training in a culture other than one's own.

111   Besides enjoying the kind of communication among young men of different provinces and regions that leads to a true sense of the universality of the Society, our members in formation should have suitable contacts, arranged with prudence, with young people of their own age—clerics, religious, laity—both of their own and other nations, so that, ridding themselves of nationalism and every other form of particularism, they will acquire the universality of mind and the openness toward different forms of cultures, diverse civilizations, and differing mentalities that our apostolic vocation demands.

For Prayer, Reflection, and Discussion

I let the Lord show me through my reactions to these texts how he wants the Society to develop. Perhaps I remember some of the formative experiences I have had that enflesh the norms spelled out in the above texts. Perhaps I regret not having some of the experiences mentioned. What is the Lord revealing to me (us) about our way of proceeding through my reactions?

WEEK V, DAY 4

While Ignatius here writes specifically about the colleges, we can extrapolate to all our formation and apostolic houses what is said here about Jesuit governance. In the mystical vision of Ignatius, the Society is hierarchically organized; the superior general, as is stated in the vow formula for profession, stands in the place of God for us. He has all authority, which he delegates to others for the good of the particular house, of the province, and of the whole Society. Our way to God and our way of carrying out God's project in this world are through this hierarchical organization.

Preparation for Prayer: see p. 3 of this volume.

What do I desire? That God give me (us) a profound appreciation of our way of proceeding, especially with regard to the place of superiors in our lives.

The Government of the Colleges
Constitutions, Part IV, Chapter 10

[419]   1. In accordance with the bulls of the Apostolic See, the Professed Society will hold the superintendency over the colleges. For since it may not seek any gain from the fixed revenues nor employ them for itself, it may be expected in the long run to proceed with greater disinterestedness and a more spiritual attitude in regard to what ought to be provided in the colleges for the greater service of God our Lord and for the good government of the colleges.

[420]   2. Except for what pertains to the Constitutions, and to suppression or alienation of such colleges, all the authority, the administration, and in general the execution of this superintendency will be vested in the superior general. He, keeping his mind fixed on the end of the colleges and of the entire Society, will see best what is expedient for them.

[421]   3. Therefore the general, by himself or through another to whom he delegates his authority in this matter, will appoint one . . . in the Society as the rector who is to have the principal charge. This rector will give account of his charge to the provincial or to whomever the general designates. The general will likewise have power to remove the rector, or to change him from this charge, as seems better to him in our Lord.

[423]   4. Care should be taken that the rector be a man of great example, edification, and mortification of all his evil inclinations, and especially a man of proven obedience and humility. He ought likewise to be discreet, fit for governing, experienced both in matters of business and of the spiritual life. He should know how to blend severity with kindness at the proper times. He should be solicitous, stalwart under work, a man of learning, and, finally, one in whom the higher superiors can confide and to whom they can with security delegate their authority. For the greater this delegated authority will be, the better will the colleges be governed to the greater divine glory.

For Prayer, Reflection, and Discussion

I ask the Lord to help me to understand the mind and heart of Ignatius. What are my reactions to the text? What have been my experiences with superiors? Do I feel that I have found God through obedience? Do I feel that the Society's choice of superiors has been in accord with the spirit of the text?

Week V, Day 5

This text continues Ignatius's directives about governance. First we read of the role of the rector and then of the attitudes of obedience expected in the rector and in his men. In addition, we note the flexibility of Ignatius in allowing the rector to interpret the Constitutions according to particular times, places, and circumstances.

Preparation for Prayer: see p. 3 of this volume.

What do I desire? That God give me (us) a profound appreciation of our way of proceeding, of our pathway to God.

The Government of the Colleges, *continued*
Constitutions, Part IV, Chapter 10

[424]   5. The function of the rector will be first of all to sustain the whole college by his prayer and holy desires, and then to see that the Constitutions are observed *[B]*. He should watch over all his subjects with great care, and guard them against difficulties from within or without the house by forestalling the difficulties or remedying them if they have occurred, in a way conducive to the good of the individuals and to that of all. He should strive to promote their progress in virtues and learning, and care for their health and for the temporal goods both stable and movable. He should appoint officials discreetly, observe how they proceed, and retain them in office or change them as he judges appropriate in the Lord. In general he ought to see to it that what has been stated about the colleges in the preceding chapters is observed.

He should fully maintain the subordination he ought to keep not only toward the superior general but also to the provincial superior, informing and having recourse to him in the matters of greater moment and following his directions since he is his superior, as it is right that those in his own college should act toward him. These ought to hold him in great respect and reverence as one who holds the place of Christ our Lord, leaving to him with true obedience the free disposal of themselves and their affairs, not keeping anything closed to him, not even their own conscience. Rather, as has been stated in the *Examen* [93–97], they should manifest their conscience to him at fixed times, and more frequently when there is reason, without showing any repugnance or any manifestations of contrary opinion, so that by union of opinion and will and by proper submission they may be better preserved and make greater progress in the divine service.

[425]   *B. Thus, just as it will pertain to the rector to see that the Constitutions are observed in their entirety, so it will be his to grant exemptions from them with authority from his own superiors (when he judges that such would be the intention*

of the one who enacted them, in a particular case according to occurrences and necessities and while keeping his attention fixed on the greater common good).

For Prayer, Reflection, and Discussion

I ask the Lord to help me to understand and to desire the profound trust in the Society and its superiors required by Jesuit obedience. What are my reactions to this text and to its underlying demands? What have been my experiences of superiors? My experiences of being a superior? Have I seen the ideal approached in my life and experience? Do I have some sense of what made such experiences possible, both in me and in the superior?

WEEK V, DAY 6

This text can serve as a summary of the motivations for the Society's decision to take on schools.

Preparation for Prayer: see p. 3 of this volume.

What do I desire? That God give me (us) a profound appreciation of our way of proceeding, an appreciation, in other words, of God's project in inspiring Ignatius and the first companions to found the Society of Jesus.

Recapitulation
The Acceptance of Universities
Constitutions, Part IV, Chapter 11

[440]   1. The same considerations of charity by which colleges are accepted, in which public classes are held for the improvement in learning and in living both of our own members and even more of those outside the Society, can extend also to accepting charge of universities in which these benefits may be spread more universally, both through the subjects which are taught and the numbers of persons who attend and the degrees which are conferred, so that

the recipients may teach with authority elsewhere what they have learned well in these universities for the glory of God our Lord.

For Prayer, Reflection, and Discussion

What struck me most forcibly during this week? What do I want to talk over with my group?

WEEK VI, DAY 1

This text introduces the issue of grades in the Society. Grades have been a bone of contention almost since the founding. We have another chance to come to terms with the issue. Our pathway to God is not always smooth. In the text the word "brothers" is added in accord with a footnote referring to the Complementary Norms.

Preparation for Prayer: see p. 3 of this volume.
What do I desire? That God give me (us) a profound appreciation of our way of proceeding with regard to grades.

Admission or Incorporation into the Society:
Who Should Admit, and When
Constitutions, Part V, Chapter 1

[510] 1. Those who have been tested in the Society sufficiently and for a time long enough that both parties may know each other and if their remaining in it is conducive to the greater service and glory of God our Lord, ought to be admitted—not to probation as was the case in the beginning, but more intrinsically as members of one same body of the Society *[A]*. This is the case chiefly with those who are admitted to profession or into the ranks of the formed coadjutors. But since the approved scholastics [and brothers] too are admitted in a different and more intrinsic manner than those received into the probation, in this Fifth Part we shall also state what we think in our Lord ought to be observed about the admission of these scholastics [and brothers].

[511]   *A. The Society, in the broadest sense of the term, includes all those who live under obedience to its superior general. Thus it comprises even the novices and the persons who, desiring to live and die in the Society, are in probation to be admitted into it under one of the other categories of membership about to be described.*

In the second and less universal sense, the Society includes not only the professed and the formed coadjutors but also the approved scholastics [and brothers]. For the body of the Society is composed of these three kinds of parts or members.

In the third and more proper sense, the Society comprises the professed and the formed coadjutors. This is the sense which is understood in regard to that entrance into the Society which the scholastics promise; that is, they promise to become either professed or formed coadjutors in the Society.

The fourth and most proper meaning of this name, the Society, comprehends only the professed. The reason is, not that the body of the Society contains no other members, but that the professed are the principal members, some of whom, as will be explained later, have active and passive voice in the election of the superior general and in other such matters.

No matter in which one of these four categories one finds himself in the Society, he is capable of sharing in the spiritual favors which, according to the grant of the Apostolic See, the superior general may dispense in the Society for the greater glory of God. Now admission to the Society in the first sense is the same as reception into probation, and has thus already been discussed above in Part I. This Fifth Part, therefore, deals with the subsequent three kinds of admission.

For Prayer, Reflection, and Discussion

I ask the Lord for his help in understanding the mind and heart of Ignatius in introducing grades into the Society. What reactions do I have as I contemplate this text? What reactions do I have as I remember my own experience and that of others during my time in the Society? What is God telling me (us) by these reactions? Can I discern what is for my (and our) peace with regard to this vexed issue?

Ignatius wanted the Society to be very careful about admission to vows. Hence the general alone has the authority to admit to vows. According to the Complementary Norms, the general habitually delegates to provincials the authority to admit to first vows, but may not easily delegate to anyone the authority to admit to solemn profession. This text faces us with the selectivity of the Society in admitting members. Reflection on the requirements for final vows will indicate how selective Ignatius wanted the Society to be because of the nature of our vocation.

Preparation for Prayer: see p. 3 of this volume.

What do I desire? That God give me (us) a profound appreciation of our way of proceeding, especially with regard to the selectivity of the Society.

Admission into the Society, *continued*

Constitutions, Part V

[512]   2. First of all, the authority to admit into the body of the Society those who ought to be admitted will be vested in whoever may be its head, as reason requires. But since the superior general cannot be everywhere, he may communicate to other members of the Society as much of his authority as seems good to him for the welfare of the entire body of the Society .

Those to Be Admitted to First Vows

Complementary Norms, Part V, Chapter 2

117   §1. For a man to be admitted to first vows, he must be considered suited to living the life of the Society and to carrying out its ministry and offices; therefore, no one is to be admitted unless, after legitimately completing two years of novitiate and undergoing the examination prescribed in the Constitutions, both he himself and the Society are satisfied.

§2. However, if he is satisfied but the Society has doubts about his aptitude, the novitiate can be extended until both parties are clearly satisfied in the Lord.

1° Provincials can extend the novitiate for six months;

2° If a further extension seems to be required for truly serious reasons, the matter is to be proposed to the general, who can permit it.

The Qualities of Those Who Should Be Admitted
Constitutions, Part V, Chapter 2

[516] 1. Inasmuch as no one should be admitted into any of the aforementioned categories who has not been judged suitable in our Lord, those persons will be judged suited for admission to profession whose life is well-known through long and thorough probations and is approved by the superior general, to whom a report will be sent by the subordinate superiors or others from whom the general desires information.

For this purpose, it will be helpful for those who had been sent to studies, upon finishing the work and effort of intellectual formation, to apply themselves during the period of final probation to the school of the heart, exercising themselves in spiritual and corporal pursuits which can engender in them greater humility, abnegation of all sensual love and will and judgment of their own, and also greater knowledge and love of God our Lord; so that when they themselves have made progress, they can better help others to progress for the glory of God our Lord.

Those to Be Admitted to Final Vows
Complementary Norms, Part V, Chapter 3

120   In the case of all who are to be admitted to last vows, they must be outstanding in the following of Christ proposed to us in the Gospels, since this is the ultimate norm of religious life; such men are those who

1° Regularly and for the most part, in ordinary matters, act according to the demands of virtue that is rooted in love of Christ, and there is firm hope that they will do the same in more difficult matters if such are encountered;

2° Humbly accept corrections concerning faults they have committed in religious life and generously strive to correct them;

3° Driven on by love, live more and more for Christ and his Body which is the Church, and in the daily practice of virtue bear witness both to our members and to others of the new life gained through the redemption of Christ.

121   For someone to be admitted to the solemn profession of four vows the following are required:

1° An outstanding level of virtue in conformity with no. 120, one that is positively demonstrated and is so obvious that the individual stands out by reason of his good example to others. A deficiency in this regard cannot be supplied by any other endowments.

2° Sound judgment and prudence in action, as well as basic virtue tested and necessary.

3° A more-than-average talent for our ministries, demonstrated for at least three years.

4° Complete availability and mobility for missions and ministries of the Society.

5° Sufficient physical and psychological health.

6° An outstanding level of learning in sacred studies or other outstanding endowments from God in conformity with §§2 and 3 below.

7° Priestly ordination.

§2. The high level of learning in sacred sciences must be shown by a higher academic degree, at least the licentiate, or by having taught them or written about them with distinction, or by the examination for grade according to no. 93, §§1 and 2.

§3. For other outstanding endowments from God (mentioned in §1, 6, above) those men can be promoted who exhibit outstanding apostolic or ministerial capability for any post or ministry proper to the Society, demonstrated respectively by having earned higher academic degrees or by having exercised the ministry for at least three years (see §1, 3, above), and always presupposing that adequate theological learning commonly required by the Church in a well-educated priest.

§4. Major superiors and their consultors must have proof that candidates proposed for profession of four vows have all the qualifications required for it.

123   No men should be admitted to final simple vows unless

1° They are outstanding in virtue in conformity with no. 120;

2° They have shown sufficient knowledge and talent for the works and ministries that are proper to the Society;

3° In the case of spiritual coadjutors, they have received ordination to the priesthood or, in the exceptional case mentioned in no. 124, ordination to the permanent diaconate.

WEEK VI, DAY 3

The name tertianship, as we know, derives from the fact that it is the "third probation," the first and second being respectively the time of postulancy and the time of novitiate. Ignatius, it seems, derived the idea of this "third probation" from the experience of the first companions in Venice after they had finished their studies in Paris. In his Autobiography *Ignatius describes a bit of this experience.*

> *In that year no ships sailed for the East because the Venetians had broken off with the Turks. So, seeing that their hope of sailing was put off, they dispersed within the Venetian region, with the intention of waiting the year they had decided upon; and if it expired without possibility of travel, they would go to Rome.*

> *It fell to the pilgrim to go with Faber and Laínez to Vicenza. There they found a certain house outside the city, which had neither doors nor windows. They stayed in it, sleeping on a little straw that they had brought. Two of them always went out to seek alms in the city twice a day, but they got so little that they could hardly maintain themselves. They usually ate a little toasted bread when they had it, and the one who remained at home saw to its toasting. In this way they spent forty days, not engaging in anything other than prayer.*

> *After the forty days, Master Jean Codure arrived; and the four together decided to begin to preach. The four went to different piazzas and began to preach on the same day and at the same hour, first shouting loudly and summoning the people with their caps. . . .*

*During the time he was at Vicenza, he had many spiritual visions
and many quite regular consolations; the contrary happened when he
was in Paris. In all that traveling he had great supernatural
experiences like those he used to have when he was in Manresa,
especially when he began to prepare for the priesthood in Venice and
when he was preparing to say Mass.*[6]

*Ignatius experienced a return to the kind of devotion that he had had before
his student days in Paris. He believed that this "third probation" would
provide a similar renewal of devotion for Jesuits prior to final vows.*

Preparation for Prayer: see p. 3 of this volume.

What do I desire? That God give me (us) a profound appreciation of our way
of proceeding.

Complementary Norms, Part V
On Tertianship

125 §1. All members before pronouncing final vows must complete
the third year of probation, exercising themselves in the school of the
heart. For priests this is not to be deferred beyond three years after
priestly ordination except for a just reason in the judgment of the provincial.

§2. The purpose of this probation is for each one, in concrete and
personal contact with the things of the Society, to bring to completion a
synthesis of spiritual, apostolic, and intellectual or technical formation,
which makes for the fuller integration in the Lord of the whole
personality, in keeping with the Society's objective as St. Ignatius
described it: "that, since they themselves have made progress, they may
better help others to make spiritual progress to the glory of God and of
our Lord."

126 Third probation should be made according to a program suitable
for attaining these ends and approved by the general; in it experiments
prescribed by the Constitutions should be diligently carried out and a
study of the Institute and our way of proceeding should be fostered with
great care.

127 A provincial can dispense no one from making a complete tertianship. It is for the general, however, to judge whether for most serious
reasons someone should be exempted from some part of it; but he will
scarcely ever dispense someone from all of it.

---

[6] Divarkar, *Pilgrim's Testament,* 137-38.

WEEK VI, DAY 4

We revisit the vow formulas, at least one of which each of us has pronounced. Note that Ignatius saw the superior general as "holding the place of God." Once again we meet the issue of grades in the Society, and the spirit with which Ignatius proposed that we accept our grade. The pronouncing of these vows requires an enormous trust in the grace of God and in the Society as the way to God.

Preparation for Prayer: see p. 3 of this volume.

What do I desire? That God give me (us) a profound appreciation of the Constitutions as our pathway to God and to the service of God's people.

Formulas for Vows in the Society of Jesus

Constitutions, Part V

The Formula for Profession of Four Vows

[527]   3. "I, N., make profession, and I promise to Almighty God, in the presence of his Virgin Mother, the whole heavenly court, and all those here present, and to you, Reverend Father N., superior general of the Society of Jesus and the one holding the place of God, and to your successors (or, to you, Reverend Father N., representing the superior general of the Society of Jesus and his successors and holding the place of God), perpetual poverty, chastity, and obedience; and, in conformity with it, special care for the instruction of children *[B]*, according to the manner of living contained in the apostolic letters of the Society of Jesus and in its Constitutions.

"I further promise a special obedience to the sovereign pontiff in regard to the missions *[C]*, according to the same apostolic letters and the Constitutions.

"Rome, or elsewhere, on such a day, month, and year, and in such a church."

[528] *B. The promise to instruct children and uneducated persons in conformity with the apostolic letters and the Constitutions does not induce a greater obligation than the other spiritual exercises by which the neighbor is aided, such as confessions, preaching, and the like. Each one ought to employ himself in these as directed by the commands of his superiors. But the promise about the children is placed in the vow so that this holy practice may be held as something more especially enjoined and may be exercised with greater devotion, in view of the special service thereby given to God our Lord in aid of his souls and the greater danger of its being allowed to fall into oblivion and dropped than is the case with other more conspicuous services such as preaching and the like.*

[529] *C. The entire purport of this fourth vow of obedience to the pope was and is with regard to missions; and this is how the bulls should be understood where they speak of this obedience in all that the sovereign pontiff may command and wherever he may send one, and so on.*

The Formula for Final Vows of Spiritual and Temporal Coadjutors

[535] 2. "I, N., promise to Almighty God, in the presence of his Virgin Mother and the whole heavenly court, and to you, Reverend Father N., superior general of the Society of Jesus and the one holding the place of God, and to your successors (or, to you, Reverend Father N., representing the superior general of the Society of Jesus and his successors and holding the place of God), perpetual poverty, chastity, and obedience; and, in conformity with it, special care for the instruction of children, according to the manner indicated in the apostolic letters and Constitutions of the aforementioned Society.

"Rome, or elsewhere, in such a place, day, month, year, and so forth."

[537] The procedure for the temporal coadjutors will be the same, with the reference to the instruction of children omitted.

The Formula for First Vows after Novitiate

[540] 4. "Almighty and eternal God, I, N., though altogether most unworthy in your divine sight, yet relying on your infinite goodness and mercy and moved with a desire of serving you, in the presence of the most holy Virgin Mary and your whole heavenly court, vow to your Divine Majesty perpetual poverty, chastity, and obedience in the Society of Jesus; and I promise that I shall enter that same Society *[E]* in order to lead my entire life in it, understanding all things according to its Constitutions. Therefore I suppliantly beg your immense Goodness and Clemency, through the blood of Jesus Christ, to deign to receive this holocaust in an odor of sweetness; and that just as you

gave me the grace to desire and offer this, so you will also bestow abundant grace to fulfill it.

"Rome, or elsewhere, in such a place, day, month, year, and so forth."

[541]   E. *The promise to enter the Society, as was stated in the beginning [511], means: to become one of its professed or its formed coadjutors, according to what its general judges to be for greater service to God.*

[542]   5. After anyone has been incorporated into the Society in one grade, he should not seek to pass to another, but should strive to perfect himself in the first one and to serve and glorify God our Lord in it, leaving the care of everything else to the superior whom he holds in place of Christ our Lord.

For Prayer, Reflection, and Discussion

I ask the Lord to help me to relive the memory of my vow day(s). What are my reactions now to these memories? To these formulas? Do I sense that God is still offering me the graces I desired when I pronounced my vows? Do I have the same trust in the Society that I had when I pronounced my vows? A deeper trust? less trust? What do I make of my reactions?

WEEK VI, DAY 5

The professed pronounce five simple vows in the sacristy immediately after the Mass during which they pronounce their solemn, public vows. The Complementary Norms here explicate the meaning of these vows. Reflection on the vows and their explication again gives us a chance to deepen our grasp of our way of proceeding. Given the history of the Society and the ways in which our vocation has brought us into the heart of cultural, political, and ecclesial life, we can better understand the prescience of Ignatius in proposing these vows as a way to keep the Society on the alert for temptations to greed and to ambition.

Preparation for Prayer: see p. 3 of this volume.

What do I desire? That God give me (us) a profound appreciation of the Constitutions as our pathway to God and to the service of God's people.

Formulas for Vows in the Society of Jesus, *continued*

Complementary Norms, Part V, Chapter 5

The Simple Vows of the Solemnly Professed

137   §1. The matter of the vow not to relax poverty, reserved to the Holy See, is completely defined in this statement of the Constitutions: "To alter what touches upon poverty would be to mitigate it by allowing some fixed revenue or possession for personal use, or for the sacristy, or for the building, or for some other purpose, apart from what pertains to the colleges and houses of probation." Therefore, in virtue of the vow the solemnly professed are obliged only to this: not to grant a stable income or any possession for its own use to houses and churches, notwithstanding other more general expressions that are found in the same declaration of the Constitutions.

§2. This practice of poverty is now applied to all apostolic communities as distinct from institutions, according to the norm of no. 191, §1.

138   In regard to the second vow of not ambitioning prelacies or, what comes to the same thing, dignities in the Society, prelacies are understood to mean the office of General, Vicar General, Provincial, Superior of a Region (or Mission), even a dependent one, and Local Superior.

139   §1. The third vow, also reserved to the Holy See, not to ambition or accept prelacies or dignities outside the Society extends to the episcopate and to the office of Vicar General and Episcopal Vicar; but not to the office of Judicial Vicar or Officialis and to Diocesan Judge nor to lay prelacies.

§2. In regard to accepting the office of Vicar General and Episcopal Vicar, the superior general, by a faculty received from the Holy See, can grant a dispensation in particular cases.

§3. In regard to accepting the episcopal office, the first response on the part of the one whose appointment is being proposed should always be to make a representation of our vow. This can more easily be done, since the Holy See does not impose an episcopal appointment without the consent of the candidate. But if in a particular case the Holy See insists or some member remains anxious because he has not positively responded immediately to the will of the Holy Father expressly manifested to him, he should refer the matter either directly or through his provincial to the superior general, so that together they may examine the more appropriate way of responding to what is proposed, according to the spirit of our Institute and for the greater glory of God.

140 The actions that are prohibited by the second and third simple vow of the solemnly professed are to be understood as external acts.

141 The fourth vow of denouncing anyone who is ambitioning honors obliges one to make a denunciation even though the one who is ambitioning is not solemnly professed.

142 The fifth vow concerns listening to the superior general, by which the one making the vow promises that if he should be promoted to the episcopate, he would not refuse to listen to the counsel which the general himself or someone else of the Society whom he substitutes for himself would see fit to give him.

For Prayer, Reflection, and Discussion

I ask the Lord to help me to grasp the mind and heart of Ignatius in requiring the professed Jesuits to pronounce these five simple vows. What are my own reactions to them? To the dangers foreseen by Ignatius?

WEEK VI, DAY 6

As we know, in Rome the companions soon found themselves having to decide about their future. In their "Deliberatio" they decided that God was calling them to start a new religious order called the Society of Jesus. The text below is put here for our prayer and reflection as we finish the week devoted to vows in the Society of Jesus. We, too, have prayed to be put under the standard of Jesus, and our vows have been a response to our conviction that God has answered our prayer.

Preparation for Prayer: see p. 3 of this volume.

What do I desire? That God give me (us) a profound appreciation of the Constitutions as our pathway to God and to the service of God's people.

Recapitulation
Ignatius's Vision at La Storta As Described
by Joseph Tylenda

This journey to Rome was Ignatius's final cross-country journey and the three pilgrims [Ignatius, Favre and Laínez] . . . approached Rome by the Via Cassia; about eight miles outside the city they came to the small village of La Storta. Since they were tired, but at the same time eager to get to Rome that evening, they chose to stop at the chapel, get some rest, do some praying, and then continue their way. When Ignatius relates the mystical experience that was his at La Storta, he merely gives the basic fact and omits all detail and embellishment. But from those who were with him we learn that as soon as Ignatius entered the chapel he felt a sudden change come over him, and while he was praying he had a remarkable vision. Both Father and Son were looking most kindly upon him and he heard the Father say to the Son: "I wish you to take him as your servant." Jesus then directed His words to the kneeling pilgrim and said: "I wish you to be our servant." This was exactly what Ignatius had always wanted. Then he heard the Father add: "I will be favorable to you in Rome." This was God's answer to Ignatius's frequent prayer that he be placed next to Mary's Son. Leaving the chapel and continuing his way to Rome, Ignatius did not know whether he would meet success or persecution, but he knew that God would be with him.[7]

For Prayer, Reflection, and Discussion

I ask the Lord to help me to deepen my appreciation of our way of proceeding with regard to grades and to first and final vows. I also take the time to reflect on the whole week with a view to what I will share with my group.

---

[7] *A Pilgrim's Journey: The Autobiography of Ignatius of Loyola,* trans. with introduction and commentary by Joseph N. Tylenda (Wilmington, Del.: Michael Glazier, 1985), 113.

WEEK VII, DAY 1

Parts VI through X deal with the formed Society, taking up in order the personal life of Jesuits, the mission of Jesuits, the union of minds and hearts, the superior general, and the preservation and well-being of the Society. Today we begin Part VI of the Constitutions regarding the personal life of Jesuits who have pronounced vows. This section of the Complementary Norms introduces Part VI and is a general statement of the rationale of our vows of poverty, chastity, and obedience.

Preparation for Prayer: see p. 3 of this volume.

What do I desire? That God give me (us) a profound appreciation of the Constitutions as our pathway to God and to the service of God's people.

The Personal Life of Those Already Admitted and Incorporated into the Body of the Society
Constitutions, Part VI, Chapter 1

[547]   1. In order that those already admitted to profession or as formed coadjutors may be able to employ themselves more fruitfully according to our Institute in the service of God and the aid of their neighbors, they need to observe certain things in regard to themselves. And although the most important of these are reduced to the vows which they offer to God our Creator and Lord in conformity with the apostolic letters, nevertheless, in order that these points may be further explained and commended, they will be treated in this present Part VI.

The Apostolic Character of Our Vows in General
Complementary Norms, Part VI, Section 1

143   §1. Our consecration by profession of the evangelical counsels, by which we respond to a divine vocation, is at one and the same time the following of Christ poor, virginal, and obedient and a rejection of those idols that the world is always prepared to adore, especially wealth, pleasure, prestige, and power. Hence, our poverty, chastity, and obedience ought visibly and efficaciously to bear witness to this attitude, whereby we proclaim the evangelical possibility of a certain communion among men and women that is a foretaste of the future kingdom of God.

§2. Our religious vows, while binding us, also set us free:

▶ free, by our vow of poverty, to share the life of the poor and to use whatever resources we may have, not for our own security and comfort, but for service

▶ free, by our vow of chastity, to be "men for others," in friendship and communion with all, but especially with those who share our mission of service

▶ free, by our vow of obedience, to respond to the call of Christ as made known to us by him whom the Spirit has placed over the Church, and to follow the lead of all our superiors

---

For Prayer, Reflection, and Discussion

I ask the help of the Lord to have an interior grasp of his call to me (and us) to pronounce these particular vows. How do I react to this text? Do the vows free me in the way described? Do I have concrete experiences of such freeing? If I do not feel freed, what will help me to experience such freedom? Do I desire such freedom?

WEEK VII, DAY 2

Obviously, recent general congregations have felt the necessity of saying more about the vow of chastity than did Ignatius in the Constitutions. Because of the changed cultural circumstances we need to have more guidance about this vow. In addition, because of the changed cultural circumstances we need to talk more openly with one another about our experience of living out the vows in order to help one another to live integrally. Moreover, we need to come to trust one another in these changed circumstances. We can best do this if we talk openly with at least some of our fellow Jesuits about our experiences of chastity. In addition to greater cultural openness, if not outright lack of restraints, about sexuality and its various expressions, we also experience much more openness about sexual orientation, at least in the United States. These changed circumstances make the prayer and sharing of this week of our enterprise very important for our life together.

Preparation for Prayer: see p. 3 of this volume.

What do I desire? That God give me (us) a profound appreciation of Jesuit apostolic chastity.

The Vow of Chastity
Constitutions, Part VI

[547]   What pertains to the vow of chastity requires no interpretation, since it is evident how perfectly it should be preserved, by endeavoring to imitate therein the purity of the angels in cleanness of body and mind.

Chastity
Complementary Norms, Part VI, Section 2

144   §1. By the vow of chastity, we devote ourselves to the Lord and to his service in such a unique love that it excludes marriage and any other exclusive human relationship, as well as the genital expression and gratification of sexuality. Thus the vow entails the obligation of complete continence in celibacy for the sake of the kingdom of heaven. Following the evangelical counsel of chastity, we aspire to deepen our familiarity with God, our configuration to Christ, our companionship with our brother Jesuits, our service to our neighbors whoever they may be; and at the same time we aspire to grow in our personal maturity and capacity to love.

§2. Hence in the Society chastity, which is before all else God's gracious gift, is essentially apostolic and the source of radical availability and mobility for mission, and not at all to be understood as directed exclusively to our own personal sanctification. Its precious apostolic fruitfulness, besides providing freedom for greater mobility in God's service, in imitation of the angels, is a mature, simple, anxiety-free dealing with the men and women with whom and for whom we exercise our ministry for building up the body of Christ.

§3. Especially in our times, when people tend to put whole classes of their fellow human beings beyond the margins of their concern, while at the same time identifying love with eroticism, the self-denying love that is warmly human, yet freely given in service to all, especially to the poor and the marginalized, can be a powerful sign leading people to Christ, who came to show us what love really is, namely, that God is love.

145   This consecration of ourselves to Christ involves a certain affective renunciation and solitude of heart; namely, a renunciation of conjugal intimacy and the possibility of having children of one's own, and of an affective bonding that is a normal condition for achieving human growth and establishing a family of one's own. But this is part of the cross offered to us by Jesus Christ as we follow his footsteps, and closely associates us with his paschal mystery and makes us sharers of the

spiritual fruitfulness that flows from it. But not only does it not diminish our personality or hamper human contacts and dialogue, it expands affectivity instead, assists people fraternally, and brings them to a fuller charity.

For Prayer, Reflection, and Discussion

I ask the Lord to help me to grasp in a profound way that he has called me to this way of life, this path to him and to service of his people. How do I react to these texts? What has been my experience of living the vow of chastity? Have I experienced the vow of chastity as a gift of God to me? Have I experienced the greater availability that the text speaks of? What are my feelings about my brothers in Christ with regard to this vow? What is the Lord revealing to me and us as we pray about this vow?

WEEK VII, DAY 3

In this section the Complementary Norms offer the Society means toward the integral living of the vow of chastity. The reference to Ignatius's experience reminds us of his words in the Autobiography *where he describes an experience of Our Lady's presence during his convalescence in Loyola:*

> *And so he began to forget the previous thoughts, with these holy desires he had, and they were confirmed by a spiritual experience, in this manner. One night while he was awake, he saw clearly an image of Our Lady with the holy Child Jesus. From this sight he received for a considerable time very great consolation, and he was left with such loathing for his whole past life, and especially for the things of the flesh, that it seemed to him that his spirit was rid of all the figures that had been printed on it. Thus from that hour until August '53, when this was written, he never gave the slightest consent to the things of the flesh. For this reason it may be considered the work of God, although he did not dare to claim it nor said more than to affirm the above. But his brother as well as all the rest of the house-*

hold came to know from his exterior the change that had been wrought inwardly in his soul.[8]

It is instructive to realize that Ignatius sees the hand of God in this experience because of its effects on him. He seems well aware that only God can enable him to live a life of chastity.

Preparation for Prayer: see p. 3 of this volume.

What do I desire? That God give me (us) a profound appreciation of Jesuit apostolic chastity.

The Vow of Chastity, *continued*

Complementary Norms, Part VI

146   §1. That the love once consecrated by chastity may grow unceasingly, all should before all else cultivate intimate familiarity with God and friendship with Christ through contemplation of his mysteries and through life-giving assimilation to him in the sacraments both of penance and of the Eucharist.

§2. It is also very important, as the Society has learned from the experience of Ignatius himself, to renew incessantly the strong desire of persevering, by means of humble and simple devotion to the Blessed Virgin Mary, who by her chaste assent obtained divine fecundity and became the mother of fair love.

§3. Chastity is more safely preserved "when in common life true fraternal love thrives among its members," by fostering charity and the ready union of souls, which disposes us to bear one another's burdens; and when we feel a generous love for one and all and at the same time engage in a helpful and fruitful dialogue with all and are true brothers and friends in Christ, leading the community life proper to the Society, as described in Part VIII, nos. 311–30.

For Prayer, Reflection, and Discussion

I ask God's help to relive my own history of living in accordance with this vow and to recall the helps of grace that have come my way through prayer and through community life. How do I react to these texts? Do I sense in myself a deep desire to be chaste not only in body but also in mind and heart?

---

[8] Divarkar, *Pilgrim's Testament,* 10-11.

The Complementary Norms continue to point out to us the means of living an integral life.

Preparation for Prayer: see p. 3 of this volume.

What do I desire? That God give me (us) a profound appreciation of Jesuit apostolic chastity.

The Vow of Chastity, *continued*

Complementary Norms, Part VI

147   §1. With humble awareness that love consecrated by chastity must constantly grow in order to come to maturity, we should use all the supernatural and natural helps available for this. Among these, however, we prefer those that are positive, such as probity of life, generous dedication to one's assigned task, great desire for the glory of God, zeal for solid virtues and spiritual concerns, openness and simplicity in dealing with and consulting with superiors, rich cultural attainments, spiritual joy, and above all true charity.

§2. We should know how to participate with moderation in the human contacts that our ministry involves, our visits and recreations, our reading and study of problems, our attendance at shows, and our use of what is pleasurable, so that our consecration to God through chastity may be strengthened and its testimony may shine forth inviolate.

§3. Also in order to foster this, our men should take into account the differing sensibilities of various cultures and, according to the custom of different places where they deal with individual persons, they should take appropriate steps with a view to the edification of all. It is especially important that those in ministries like spiritual direction or counseling keep appropriate "professional boundaries."

§4. Nevertheless, mindful of our frailty, which throughout our whole life accompanies the development of chaste love, we cannot omit observance of the ascetical norms confirmed by the Church and the Society in their wide experience and required by today's dangers to chastity. These include, above all, examination of conscience, spiritual direction, internal self-discipline, and custody of the senses, by which with the help of God's grace we diligently moderate desires and impulses that might lessen a just and wholesome dominion over our senses and affections.

WEEK VII, DAY 5

Preparation for Prayer: see p. 3 of this volume.

What do I desire? That God give me (us) a profound appreciation of Jesuit apostolic chastity.

The Vow of Chastity, *continued*

Complementary Norms, Part VI

148 §1. All our members should share in a common responsibility seriously to safeguard chastity and to further it through their mutual support and friendship as well as through the aid they offer superiors in their care for their companions and for the Society.

§2 Superiors and spiritual directors should

1° Manifest the utmost solicitude for the spiritual life of each individual, accompanying him dependably and helping him to overcome fatigue, difficulties, and temptations that he may experience on the path of a life dedicated to chastity.

2° See to it that our members in the course of their formation are educated and strengthened in the matter of sex in a suitable, positive, and prudent manner, so as to be able vigorously to surmount the various crises attending maturation. If serious psychological problems emerge, a member should be advised to visit a counselor, psychologist, or psychiatrist.

3° Firmly exercising true charity toward our members, take care that those who are unfit or doubtfully suitable for observing chastity are not admitted to the Society and, even more, that they are not admitted to vows or promoted to orders.

4° Solicitously, attentively, and with much trust be at the service of newly ordained priests and younger brothers who are beginning to work in the vineyard of the Lord, and also of those who for a long time engage in arduous special studies. They should lovingly endeavor to lead back those whom they see or sense to be drawing away from the community.

For Prayer, Reflection, and Discussion

Once again we give the Lord the opportunity to show us how we might help one another to live chastity integrally in our modern world. Have I experienced the help of my brothers in the living of this vow? Have I taken on the responsibility mentioned in no. 148, §1? How have I shown this responsibility? Do I sense that the Lord wants anything further from me with regard to this responsibility? How do I regard superiors? Do I entrust to them the intimate details of my struggles with chastity? Do I have a spiritual director to whom I tell the truth? What else does the Lord bring to mind as I ponder these texts?

WEEK VII, DAY 6

Preparation for Prayer: see p. 3 of this volume.

What do I desire? That God give me (us) a profound appreciation of Jesuit apostolic chastity.

Recapitulation

I go over the prayer and reflections of the previous week, asking the Lord to confirm me in my call and to lead me toward him through the living of the vows.

WEEK VIII, DAY 1

In congregations with capitular government, religious believe that God will direct them as individuals and as a group through the deliberations of the chapter, with all the imperfections of such a group. In the Society we believe that God will direct us as individuals and as a group through our relations with our superiors, sinners and imperfect though we all are. As we pray and reflect on the vow of obedience, we touch the heart of our pathway to God and to the service of God's people. The words of the Constitutions "They should keep in view God our Creator and Lord" reminds us of the words of the Formula of the Institute, "Let any such person take care, as long as he lives, first of all to keep before his eyes God and then the nature of this Institute which is, so to speak, a pathway to God."

Preparation for Prayer: see p. 3 of this volume.

What do I desire? That God give me (us) a profound appreciation and love of our way of proceeding with regard to the vow of obedience.

The Vow of Obedience
Constitutions, Part VI

[547]   All should strongly dispose themselves to observe obedience and to distinguish themselves in it, not only in the matters of obligation but also in the others, even though nothing else be perceived except an indication of the superior's will without an expressed command. They should keep in view God our Creator and Lord, for whom such obedience is practiced, and endeavor to

proceed in a spirit of love and not as men troubled by fear. Hence all of us should be eager to miss no point of perfection which we can with God's grace attain in the observance of all the Constitutions and of our manner of proceeding in our Lord, by applying all our energies with very special care to the virtue of obedience shown first to the sovereign pontiff and then to the superiors of the Society.

Consequently, in all the things into which obedience can with charity be extended, we should be ready to receive its command just as if it were coming from Christ our Savior, since we are practicing the obedience [to one] in his place and because of love and reverence for him.

Complementary Norms, Part VI

149   Impelled by love of Christ, we embrace obedience as a distinctive charism conferred by God on the Society through its founder, whereby we may be united the more surely and constantly with God's salvific will, and at the same time be made one in Christ among ourselves. Thus, through the vow of obedience our Society becomes a more fit instrument of Christ in his Church, to assist souls for God's greater glory.

For Prayer, Reflection, and Discussion

I ask the Lord to show me how he has led me (and us) through this vow. Have I found God through obedience? How? Have I experienced God in dealing with superiors? Have I experienced God as a superior? What is God revealing to me (us) about our practice of the vow of obedience?

WEEK VIII, DAY 2

Here the modern Society interprets, in the light of Ignatius's own practice and of our history, the way in which Jesuit obedience should work. In his Memoriale *Gonçalves da Câmara notes that Ignatius's practice with mortified men was to try to find out what they desired to do, believing that such men were inspired by God just as much as he was. He would then assign them to this task.*

Preparation for Prayer: see p. 3 of this volume.

What do I desire? That God give me (us) a profound appreciation and love of our way of proceeding with regard to the vow of obedience.

The Vow of Obedience, *continued*

Complementary Norms, Part VI

150 §1. Obedience is always an act of faith and freedom whereby the religious recognizes and embraces the will of God manifested to him by one who has authority to send him in the name of Christ. But both the superior who sends and the companion who is sent gain assurance that the mission is really God's will if it is preceded by special dialogue.

§2. Therefore if we are to receive and to fulfill our mission through obedience, we must be faithful to that practice of spiritual apostolic discernment, both personal and in community, so central to our way of proceeding, as rooted in the Spiritual Exercises and the Constitutions. This discernment grows and gains strength by the examination of conscience, personal prayer and brotherly dialogue within our community, and the openness to superiors through the account of conscience that inclines us toward obedience.

151 §1. All receive their mission from the superior, but the superior himself expects the community to discern in union with him and in conformity with his final decision, the concrete ways whereby that mission is to be accomplished and the procedure by which it is to be evaluated and revised in the light of actual performance.

§2. If, therefore, the question at issue is of some importance and the necessary preconditions have been verified, the use of communal and apostolic discernment is encouraged as a privileged way to find God's will.

§3. In the Society the discerning community is not a deliberative or capitular body but a consultative one, whose object, clearly understood and fully accepted, is to assist the superior to determine what course of action is for God's greater glory and the service of humankind. It is up to him to make the final decision in the light of the discernment, but freely, as the one to whom both the grace and the burden of authority are given.

WEEK VIII, DAY 3

The text of the Constitutions presents us with the stark language of Ignatius with regard to a Jesuit's inner attitude toward superiors' commands or even wishes. The Complementary Norms clarify the Constitutions without in any way watering down the bottom line. CN no. 154, not reproduced here, provides important guidelines for dealing with conflicts between a member's conscience and the demands of obedience.

Preparation for Prayer: see p. 3 of this volume.

What do I desire? That God give me (us) a profound appreciation and love of our way of proceeding with regard to the vow of obedience.

The Vow of Obedience, *continued*
Constitutions, Part VI

[547] . . . Therefore we should be ready to leave unfinished any letter or anything else of ours which we have begun, and in the Lord to bend our whole mind and energy so that holy obedience, in regard to the execution, the willing, and the understanding, may always be perfect in every detail as we perform with great alacrity, spiritual joy, and perseverance whatever has been commanded us, persuading ourselves that everything is just and renouncing with blind obedience any contrary opinion and judgment of our own in all things which the superior commands and in which (as is stated in [549]) no species of sin can be judged to be present [Clarified in *CN* 154, pp. 223, 225].

We ought to act on the principle that everyone who lives under obedience should let himself be carried and directed by Divine Providence through the agency of the superior as if he were a lifeless body, which allows itself to be carried to any place and treated in any way; or an old man's staff, which serves at any place and for any purpose in which the one holding it in his hand wishes to employ it. For in this way the obedient man ought joyfully to employ himself in any task in which the superior desires to employ him in aid of the whole body of the religious order; and he ought to hold it certain that by so doing he conforms himself with the divine will more than by anything else he could do while following his own will and different judgment.

Complementary Norms, Part VI

(a clarification of the last phrase of the section just cited)

152   In offering personal obedience, all should leave to superiors the full and completely free disposal of themselves, desiring to be guided, not by their own judgment and will, but by that indication of the divine will that is offered to us through obedience; and they should make their own the superior's command in a personal, responsible way and with all diligence "bring to the execution of commands and the discharge of assignments entrusted to them the resources of their minds and wills, and their gifts of nature and grace."

153   Obedience by its very nature and perfection supposes in the subject the obligation of personal responsibility and the spirit of ever seeking what is better. Consequently, he can, and sometimes should, set forth his own reasons and proposals to the superior. But a subject may not refuse to obey in those things where there is not manifestly any sin, because he thinks something better should be done or because he believes he is led along other lines by the inspiration of the Spirit.

For Prayer, Reflection, and Discussion

I ask the Lord to reveal to me (and us) how he wishes us to live out our way to him and to the service of his people. How does the language of the Constitutions strike me now? How did it strike me when I was a novice? What changes have occurred in our way of proceeding since I entered the Society? What is the Lord revealing to me (us) about our way of life?

The account of conscience was considered of such importance for the governance of the Society that the Society sought and received an exemption from the 1917 Code of Canon Law which forbade religious congregations from requiring the account of conscience. Yet we must admit that the practice of the account of conscience was not ideal, to put it mildly, during the years prior to GC 31. We are only gradually recovering the ideal hoped for by Ignatius.

Preparation for Prayer: see p. 3 of this volume.

What do I desire? That God give me (us) a profound appreciation and love of our way of proceeding with regard to the vow of obedience.

The Vow of Obedience, *continued*

Constitutions, Part VI

[551]   2. Likewise, it should be strongly recommended to all that they should have and show great reverence, especially interior reverence, for their superiors, by considering and reverencing Jesus Christ in them; and from their hearts they should warmly love their superiors as fathers in him. Thus in everything they should proceed in a spirit of charity, keeping nothing exterior or interior hidden from the superiors and desiring them to be informed about everything, so that the superiors may be the better able to direct them in everything along the path of salvation and perfection. For that reason, once a year and as many times more as their superior thinks good, all the professed and formed coadjutors should be ready to manifest their consciences to him {in confession [abolished]}, or in secret, or in another manner, for the sake of the great profit this practice contains, as was stated in the *Examen* [91, 92, 97].

[552]   3. All should have recourse to the superior for the things which they happen to desire; and without his permission and approval no individual should directly or indirectly request, or cause to be requested, any favor from the sovereign pontiff or from another person outside the Society, either for himself or for someone else. He should be convinced that if he does not get what he desires through the hands of the superior or with his approval, it is not useful to him for the divine service; and that if it is useful to him for that service, he will get it with the consent of the superior, as from the one who holds the place of Christ our Lord for him.

Complementary Norms, Part VI

155   §1. The account of conscience, by which the superior becomes able to take part in each one's discernment and to help him therein, is to retain intact its value and vitality as an element of great moment in the spiritual governance of the Society. Therefore, all should give an account of conscience to their superiors, according to the norms and spirit of the

Society, inspired by charity, with any obligation under pain of sin always precluded. In addition, the relationships between superiors and their brethren in the Society should be such as to encourage the manifestation of conscience and conversation about spiritual matters.

§2. No one, without exception, may directly or indirectly make known what has been revealed in an account of conscience unless it is with the express consent of the one rendering the account.

156   Ours should neither seek to have externs intercede for them with superiors nor allow this to happen in any instance.

For Prayer, Reflection, and Discussion

What has been my experience of the account of conscience? Do I see the account of conscience as an essential of Jesuit obedience? Do I speak openly and honestly to superiors? Do I have any reservations about either the theory or practice of the account of conscience? What is the Lord revealing to me (us) about our way of proceeding through my (our) reactions? Do I feel the need to make any changes in my behavior in regard to the account of conscience?

WEEK VIII, DAY 5

This text from the General Examen *once again gives Ignatius's view of obedience and in a rather stark way. Reflection on it may help us to grasp in a deeper way the mystical insight of Ignatius with regard to obedience.*

Preparation for Prayer: see p. 3 of this volume.

What do I desire? That God give me (us) a profound appreciation and love of our way of proceeding with regard to the vow of obedience.

The Vow of Obedience, *continued*

General Examen

[84]   29. When someone goes to the kitchen to do the cooking or to help him who is doing it, with great humility he must obey the cook in all things pertaining to his office, by showing him always complete obedience. For if he should not do this, neither, it seems, would he show obedience to any other superior, since genuine obedience considers, not the person to whom it is offered, but Him for whose sake it is offered; and if it is exercised for the sake of our Creator and Lord alone, then it is the very Lord of everyone who is obeyed. In no manner, therefore, ought one to consider whether it is the cook of the house who gives the order or its superior, or one person rather than another. For, to consider the matter with sound understanding, obedience is not shown either to these persons or for their sake, but to God alone and only for the sake of God our Creator and Lord.

[85]   30. Therefore it is better that the cook should not request his helper to do this or that, but that he should modestly command him by saying, "Do this" or "Do that." For if he requests him, he will seem to be speaking rather as man to man; and it does not seem right and proper for a lay cook to request a priest to clean the pots and do other similar tasks. But by commanding him or saying, "Do this" or "Do that," he will show more clearly that he is speaking as Christ to man, since he is commanding in His place. Thus the person who obeys ought to consider and heed the order which comes from the cook, or from another who is his superior, as if it were coming from Christ our Lord, so that he may be entirely pleasing to his Divine Majesty.

For Prayer, Reflection, and Discussion

What is the Lord revealing to me (us) about our vow of obedience and its practice? Do I (we) instinctively trust that God is leading us through our superiors? Do I experience myself as obeying Christ when I obey my superiors? Do I (we) need conversion in the practice of obedience?

WEEK VIII, DAY 6

Preparation for Prayer: see p. 3 of this volume.

What do I desire? That God give me (us) a profound appreciation and love of our way of proceeding with regard to the vow of obedience.

The Vow of Obedience, *continued*
Recapitulation

For Prayer, Reflection, and Discussion

What has the Lord been teaching me during the past week as I prayed and reflected on the Society's theory and practice of obedience?

WEEK IX, DAY 1

We recall that Ignatius spent forty days praying over the question of the poverty of our houses and churches. The part of his spiritual diary that is still extant is a record of his mystical experiences as he grappled with the question of poverty. He felt that God was calling the Society to the radical poverty contained in the Constitutions.[9] The Society has struggled for well over a century about how to interpret for modern times the determinations taken by Ignatius on poverty. The last few general congregations have definitively interpreted our vow of poverty, and these interpretations have been approved by the Holy See. In the texts cited here we see the motivation for the vow and the general principles.

Preparation for Prayer: see p. 3 of this volume.

---

[9] See "The Deliberation on Poverty and Selections from The Spiritual Diary," in *Ignatius of Loyola: The Spiritual Exercises and Selected Works,* ed. George E. Ganss, S.J. (New York/Mahwah: Paulist, 1991), 215-70.

What do I desire? That God give me (us) a profound appreciation and love of our way of proceeding with regard to the vow of poverty.

The Vow of Poverty
Constitutions, Part VI

[553] 1. Poverty, as the strong wall of the religious institute, should be loved and preserved in its integrity as far as this is possible with God's grace. The enemy of the human race generally tries to weaken this defense and rampart which God our Lord inspired religious institutes to raise against him and the other adversaries of their perfection. Into what was well ordered by their first founders he induces alterations by means of interpretations and innovations not in conformity with those founders' first spirit. Therefore, so that provision may be made in this matter as far as lies in our power, all those who make profession in this Society should promise not to take part in altering what pertains to poverty in the Constitutions *[A]*, unless it be in some manner to make it more strict, [see *CN* no. 137] according to the circumstances in the Lord.

[554] *A. To alter what touches upon poverty would be so to mitigate it as to have any fixed revenue or possession for personal use, or for the sacristy, or for the building, or for some other purpose, apart from what pertains to the colleges and the houses of probation [clarified by* CN *no. 137; 191, §1]. To prevent the Constitutions from being changed in so important a matter, each one after making his profession will make this promise in the presence of the superior general and those who happen to be present with him: In the sight of our Creator and Lord he will promise to take no part in altering what pertains to poverty in the Constitutions, either in a congregation assembled from the entire Society or by attempting this himself in any manner.*

Poverty: Certain General Principles
Complementary Norms, Part VI, Section 4

157 Voluntary religious poverty is the attempt of fallen human beings, in the radical following of the humble and poor Christ, to achieve that freedom from every inordinate attachment which is the condition for a great and ready love of God and neighbor.

158 The principle and foundation of our poverty is found in a love of the Word of God made flesh and crucified. Therefore in the Society that way of life is to be maintained which is as far as possible removed from all infection of avarice and as like as possible to evangelical poverty, which our first fathers experienced as more gratifying, more undefiled, and more suitable for the edification of the neighbor.

159   §1. Our poverty in the Society is apostolic: our Lord has sent us "to preach in poverty." Therefore our poverty is measured by our apostolic purpose, so that our entire apostolate is informed with the spirit of poverty.

§2. Efficiency in the apostolate and the witness of apostolic poverty are two values that are closely united and must be held in an ongoing tension; this is a rule for apostolic institutes as well as for individuals.

160   Our poverty is the condition of our apostolic credibility, as the total expression of our trust in God and our freely given service to others, when we are made witnesses of the freely bestowed love of God, who gave his Son for us in the total emptying of the incarnation and the cross.

161   The forms of our poverty must truly suit the mentality, life, and apostolate of our times and give a visible witness to the Gospel. Therefore, our contemporary poverty must be especially characterized by these qualities: sincerity, by which our lives are really poor; devotion to work, by which we resemble workers in the world; and charity, by which we freely devote ourselves and all we have for the service of the neighbor.

162   Let our poverty, sincerely and profoundly renewed, be

▸ simple in community expression and joyous in the following of Christ

▸ happy in sharing all goods among ourselves and with others

▸ apostolic in its active indifference and readiness for any service

▸ inspiring our selection of ministries and turning us to those most in need

▸ spiritually effective, proclaiming Jesus Christ in our way of life and in all we do

163   The preferential option for the poor, as proposed by the Church, which the Society wishes to make its own, should find some concrete expression directly or indirectly in the life of every companion of Jesus, as well as in the orientations of our existing apostolic works and in our choice of new ministries.

WEEK IX, DAY 2

The Complementary Norms here spell out for the individual the meaning of our vow of poverty.

Preparation for Prayer: see p. 3 of this volume.

What do I desire? That God give me (us) a profound appreciation and love of our way of proceeding with regard to the vow of poverty.

The Vow of Poverty, *continued*
The Poverty of Individuals
Complementary Norms, Part VI, Article 1

164   §1. After their first vows Ours retain ownership of their goods and the capacity to acquire other goods for themselves, but only those that constitute their patrimony or capital or pertain to it either by their very nature or by the will of the donors or for some other special reason. Other goods they acquire for the Society.

§2. They act against the vow of poverty who without permission exercise an act of proprietorship over their goods.

165   §1. Without explicit permission of the superior, Ours are sternly prohibited from

1° Accepting a loan of money from someone outside the Society, either for themselves or for another, even if it is to be spent for pious purposes

2° Investing money for profit, on any pretext whatever, in their own name or in another's, with due regard for no. 57, §2, 2

§2. The prohibition against anyone's having money either in his possession or in the possession of another includes the sort of money or other goods that some one of Ours uses as he pleases, but whose ownership, indeed, remains with someone else; no superior can permit such a practice.

§3. If on occasion just reasons seem to suggest that someone should be allowed to have money received from a person outside the Society, he should keep these funds in the possession of the superior or the treasurer. Such a deposit is always subject to the authority of superiors, with due regard for the intentions of the donors. Superiors should be careful, however, that such funds on deposit do not become in some sense permanent and that a sort of peculium is not gradually introduced.

166   §1. Our members are forbidden to accept any responsibility for administering the goods of nonmembers of the Society, even of relatives.

§2. No one except the general can grant a dispensation from this prohibition.

167   All should faithfully exercise dependence upon superiors in the use of temporal goods, both in seeking permission and in giving an account of expenditures and, where applicable, of administration.

ARTICLE 2: RENUNCIATION OF PROPERTY

168   A renunciation of goods made after first vows without permission of the superior involves a violation of the vow of poverty of the Society.

169   The renunciation before final vows should be

1° Universal, such that it embraces all goods and rights which one actually has, and any right to or control over property that could come to him

2° Absolute, such that the one making the renunciation deprives himself of all hope of recovering the goods at any time

170   The formula of renunciation should be drawn up in such language that all avenues of escape are cut off; and every required formality should be attended to, so that the renunciation will to the extent possible have its effects even in civil law.

WEEK IX, DAY 3

These texts speak of our common life, our life in community.

Preparation for Prayer: see p. 3 of this volume.

What do I desire? That God give me (us) a profound appreciation and love of our way of proceeding with regard to the vow of poverty.

The Vow of Poverty, *continued*
Constitutions, Part VI

[580]   16. What pertains to food, sleep, and the use of the other things necessary or proper for our life will be ordinary and not different from that which appears good to the physician of the place of residence *[N]*, in such a manner that what each one subtracts from this will be withdrawn through his own devotion and not through obligation. Nevertheless there should be concern for the humility, poverty, and spiritual edification which we ought to keep always in view in our Lord.

[581]   *N. In individual cases it will be left to the discretion of those in charge to provide as is fitting for the greater or smaller needs of the individual persons according to their circumstances.*

Common Life
Complementary Norms, Part VI, Article 3

174   In the Society "common life" should be understood as follows:

1° As to food, clothing, and other necessities of life, superfluities are always to be avoided and the same standard of living of different communities and of the members in them is to be maintained, insofar as differences of ministries and of places allow. But if something special is judged necessary for someone because of ill health or some other just reason, this is in no sense contrary to common life.

2° All these items superiors should provide for Ours; it is not allowed for anyone to procure these items for himself in some other way; nor may any superior give permission to do so.

3° If externs should of their own initiative offer anything of this sort, it should be accepted for common use; however, in particular cases the superior in his prudence should judge what ought to be done.

4° Since in modern life there are many procedures that can make the use of money almost invisible, all should be fully honest with superiors in the use of such means.

175   Our members who are attached to some community for reasons of study, health, or other special purposes, and those as well from another province who are not applied to this one but are attached to one of its communities, should be considered not guests but true members of the community who share fully its common life, with consequent rights and obligations according to the norm of no. 174. The provincials concerned should clearly determine whatever has to do with expenses and income, without prejudice to the requirements of common life.

ARTICLE 4: OUR COMMON WAY OF LIVING IN EXTERNAL MATTERS

176   §1. Our community poverty includes two aspects: that "common life" which St. Ignatius derived from a centuries-old tradition and current Church law still sanctions as an essential element for all religious families; and that mode of living which, in the following of Christ as he preached with the apostles, bears the mark of the special calling that ought to characterize the Society's efforts as it works among people for the redemption of the world.

§2. Moreover, it is of the utmost importance that an apostle, always following the poor Christ, in some manner accommodate himself to the manner of life of those whom he helps, becoming all things to all people. Therefore our every use of material things should be such that, by sharing these goods in common, we not only express and strengthen the unity of heart and mind of all members of the Society but also, by the tenor of our life, signify to the world our will, both common and personal, to give a witness of evangelical poverty, humbly and fraternally serving all, especially the poor, so that we may gain all for Christ, living in a manner that is poor and common in its externals.

177 The dictum in our Institute that the manner of life in the Society should be "common" and not unlike the life of "good priests in the same locality" is to be understood as follows: The Society does not assume as obligatory any austerities in the external way of life, as other institutes customarily do. The life of good priests should be understood according to the norms on evangelical and religious poverty given in nos. 160–63, 176–80.

178 §1. Our manner of living, therefore, with respect to food, clothing, habitation, recreation, vacations, travel, working facilities, and so forth should be appropriate to "disciples of the poor Christ" and not beyond what people of modest means can afford, those who must work hard to support themselves and their families. In this regard, those who have influential and well-salaried positions must be especially alert. If we must undertake travels or use equipment exceeding such limits, these must really be, and as far as possible should clearly be seen to be, means necessary for our apostolate alone, means that we employ within the limits imposed by our poverty and never as belonging to ourselves alone.

§2. Ours should not be allowed things that are unusual, unnecessary, excessively elegant, or in any way incompatible with religious poverty and simplicity. In making a journey, Ours should refrain from side trips and from expenditures that are less in keeping with our poverty, and when possible they should stay in our houses.

179 §1. The buildings of the Society should be suitable for our ministries and useful for living purposes; they should be sound and strongly built. But they ought to be such that it will be clear that we are mindful of poverty. Consequently, they should not be luxurious or too elaborate. In them, especially in the part reserved to Ours, and in any of our works, we are to avoid too exquisite a refinement and ornamentation and every type of extravagance, always keeping in mind both the purpose of our institutions and our religious poverty.

§2. It can be a great help to the simplicity and intimacy of community life as well as to poverty if the house or place where we live and the house or place where we work or even where we study can be properly separated, provided that this can be done without harm to poverty or apostolic work.

180 Unless there are evident considerations suggesting the contrary, provincials should encourage those communities which, in union and charity with the rest of the province, choose to practice a stricter poverty or to live among the poor, serving them and sharing something of their experience, in such a way that these communities may be a visible sign of the application of our option for the poor and thus may contribute by means of fraternal exchange to increasing the social sensitivity of the province. Moreover, it is recommended to all our members that in accord

with the constant tradition of the Society, they have at least some ministry with the poor.

For Prayer, Reflection, and Discussion

I ask the Lord to speak to me (us) through my reactions to these texts about our common life. What are my reactions and reflections as I ponder these norms in prayer? Perhaps this is a time for an examination of consciousness regarding our common life, and then in the small group a communal examination of consciousness. Is the Lord telling us anything about our common life through my reactions and through our sharing?

WEEK IX, DAY 4

Recent general congregations have definitively declared what the gratuity of ministries means for our time. The Complementary Norms summarize these determinations and also give the reasons for such gratuity.

Preparation for Prayer: see p. 3 of this volume.

What do I desire? That God give me (us) a profound appreciation and love of our way of proceeding with regard to the vow of poverty.

The Vow of Poverty, *continued*
Constitutions, Part VI

[565]   7. All who are under the obedience of the Society should remember that they ought to give gratuitously what they have gratuitously received [Matt. 10:9], without demanding or accepting any stipend or alms as compensation for Masses or confessions or preaching or lecturing or visiting or any other ministry among those which the Society may exercise according to our Institute *[G],* so that thus it may proceed in the divine service with greater liberty and greater edification of the neighbor.

[566]   *G. Although all those who wish may give an alms to the house or the church (whether they receive spiritual help from it or not), nothing ought to be*

accepted as a stipend or alms for what is given to them solely out of service to Christ our Lord, in such a manner that the one is given or received in exchange for the other.

[567]   8. To avoid all appearance of avarice, especially in the spiritual ministries which the Society exercises in order to aid souls, in the church there should not be a box in which those who come to the sermons, Masses, confessions, and so on customarily place their alms.

[568]   9. For the same reason, the members should not give small presents to important persons as is customarily done to elicit greater gifts from them. Neither shall they make a practice of visiting important persons of this kind, unless it is for spiritual purposes of doing good works or when the persons are so intimately benevolent in our Lord that such a service seems due to them at times.

[569]   10. The members should be ready to beg from door to door when obedience or necessity requires it. Some person or persons should be designated to request alms by which the members of the Society may be supported. These persons should ask for them with simplicity, for the love of God our Lord.

Poverty in Common

Complementary Norms, Part VI, Chapter 2

ARTICLE 1: SOURCES OF REVENUES NEEDED FOR SUPPORT AND APOSTOLATE

181   The gratuity of ministries proper to our Institute is to be explained especially from its purpose, which is both inner freedom (refraining from seeking one's own temporal advantage), outer freedom (independence from the bonds of undue obligation), and the edification of the neighbor that arises from this freedom and from the love of Christ and humankind.

182   §1. Preaching the word of God and spiritual and sacramental ministry, by which the Society carries out its purpose, of their very nature completely transcend all consideration of material remuneration and urge us toward a perfect gratuity.

§2. With the exception of the special norms for parishes and of a legitimate recompense for travel and other expenses, including sustenance, Jesuits may demand no stipend for their work in spiritual ministries, especially for those mentioned in the beginning of the *Formula of the Institute* of Julius III (1550); they may accept only those stipends that are offered to them.

183   As to the prescriptions of the Constitutions concerning the gratuity of our ministries, no superior, not even the general, can validly give a dispensation.

184   We may accept stipends or offerings given for the celebration of Mass, according to the current law of the Church. But where it can be done, gratuity should be practiced both in and outside the Society, taking account of edification of the people of God and of charity especially toward the poor.

185   In addition to the alms and income that different types of communities and apostolic institutes can accept (see nos. 191, §§2–3; 196; 199), gain from or remuneration for work done according to the Institute is also a legitimate source of material goods that are necessary for the life and apostolate of Jesuits. But we are to select these works according to the obligations of obedience and the nature of our ministries, avoiding every desire of monetary gain or temporal advantage.

186   The royalties due authors, emoluments, honoraria, personal pensions, grants, and other gifts that are considered to be the fruit of the talents and industry of Jesuits may be accepted, as also the remuneration attached to certain stable ministries, such as those of hospital chaplains, catechists, and the like.

187   With due regard for nos. 57, §2; 164, §1; 171, 1 and 6, all yearly pension payments, even small ones, that are assigned to Ours must not be used as they choose, but rather are to be applied by the provincial in accord with norms approved by the general.

For Prayer, Reflection, and Discussion

What are my reactions and reflections as I ponder these norms in prayer? Is the Lord revealing anything to me (us) through my reactions and reflections? Do I have concerns about my own or our way of proceeding with regard to any of these matters?

WEEK IX, DAY 5

The Complementary Norms definitively determine the poverty of the Society, equating apostolic communities with professed houses and requiring that apostolic institutions be separated from apostolic communities.

Preparation for Prayer: see p. 3 of this volume.

What do I desire? That God give me (us) a profound appreciation and love of our way of proceeding with regard to the vow of poverty.

The Vow of Poverty, *continued*
Constitutions, Part VI

[557]   3. The professed should live on alms in the houses (when they are not sent away on missions), {and they should not hold the ordinary office of rectors of the colleges or universities of the Society} [abolished], (unless this is necessary or notably useful for these institutions); and in the houses they should not avail themselves of the fixed revenues of these colleges.

Distinction between Communities and Apostolic Institutes
Complementary Norms, Part VI, Article 2

188   §1. Community is here taken to mean any group of Jesuits legitimately constituted under the authority of the same local superior.

§2. Apostolic institutes are those institutions or works belonging to the Society that have a certain permanent unity and organization for apostolic purposes, such as universities, colleges, retreat houses, reviews, and other activities of this kind in which our members carry on their apostolic work.

§3. All communities can have attached to them one or more apostolic institutes in which the whole community or some of its members exercise the apostolate.

189   §1. A clear distinction is to be established between communities and apostolic institutes, at least with regard to specifying the use of their goods and the profit therefrom *[ususfructus]* and between the financial accounts of each.

§2. A distinction of moral persons, canonical or civil, is also recommended where this can be effected without great inconvenience, preserving always the apostolic finality of the institutes and the authority of the Society to direct them to such ends.

ARTICLE 3: THE POVERTY OF COMMUNITIES

190   §1. Communities may be the juridical subject of all rights, including ownership, pertaining to the apostolic institutes attached to such communities.

§2. The goods of apostolic institutes of the Society may not be diverted to the use or profit of our members or communities, except for a suitable remuneration to be approved by the provincial, for work in such institutes or for services rendered to them.

191   §1. All communities dedicated to pastoral work or to any other apostolic functions are held to the practice of poverty that is indicated in the Constitutions for "houses"; and therefore, these communities are forbidden these and these only assured and permanent sources of income; namely, those that are derived from moveable and immoveable property that either belongs to the Society or is invested in foundations in such a way that the Society has a legal claim to it.

    §2. Therefore, all other forms of fixed and stable revenues are licit, such as revenues from insurance, pensions, or temporary investments permitted according to the norm of no. 195.

194   In each community, after community discernment about its lifestyle, which ought to bear credible witness to the countercultural values of the Gospel, the responsible administrators each year at the appointed times, according to norms established by the provincial and the criteria given in no. 178, should draft a projected budget as well as a statement of revenues and expenses. These will be communicated to the community as soon as convenient and are to be approved by the provincial.

195   That the life of our communities may be "removed as far as possible from all infection of avarice and conformed as closely as possible to evangelical poverty," the surplus of each community is to be distributed yearly, according to the provision of nos. 210–11, except for a moderate sum to be approved by the provincial for unforeseen expenses. This sum is never to exceed the ordinary expenses of one year.

ARTICLE 5: THE POVERTY OF APOSTOLIC INSTITUTES

199   Apostolic institutes, churches excepted, can have revenue-bearing capital and stable revenues, adequate to their purposes, if this seems necessary to the provincial.

200   §1. Superiors and directors, mindful that we are sent to preach in poverty, will take great care that our apostolic institutes avoid every manner of extravagance and limit themselves strictly to the functional, attentive to the standards of similar institutes or works of the region and to their apostolic finality.

    §2. It is the responsibility of the provincial to determine what is required so that the apostolic institutes belonging to the Society manifest this character and mark of apostolic evangelical poverty. Whether it is fitting to retain rich and powerful institutions requiring great capital resources is to be weighed prudently and spiritually.

202   If an apostolic institute is suppressed, superiors, according to their respective competence, will take care to devote its assets to another

apostolic work or place them in the fund for apostolic works of the province, of the region, or of the Society, respecting always, if this applies, the statutes of the institute and the will of benefactors. Such assets may never be diverted to the use or benefit of a community, of a province, of a region, or of the Society.

For Prayer, Reflection, and Discussion

What are my reactions and reflections as I ponder these norms in prayer? Is the Lord revealing anything to me (us) through my reactions and reflections? Do I (we) have any questions about our way of carrying out these norms? I ask the Lord to help me (us) to live an authentic Jesuit life according to the mind and heart of Ignatius.

WEEK IX, DAY 6

These texts can serve as a background for a recapitulation of this week devoted to a prayerful reflection on our way of proceeding with regard to the vow of poverty. The principles for sharing of resources are enunciated, as is the rationale for FACSI, Father General's fund for apostolic purposes to which all Jesuits are asked to contribute each Lent.

Preparation for Prayer: see p. 3 of this volume.

What do I desire? That God give me (us) a profound appreciation and love of our way of proceeding with regard to the vow of poverty.

The Vow of Poverty (recapitulation)
The Sharing of Goods
Complementary Norms, Part VI, Article 7

210   §1. According to norms to be established by the provincial and approved by Father General, there is to be provision for the distribution of the communities' surplus mentioned in no. 195, for the benefit of those communities or works of the province that are in greater need.

§2. The first beneficiary of such surplus in each community will be the apostolic institute or institutes attached to it if these stand in need, unless the provincial, with his consultors, should decide otherwise.

§3. In this sharing of resources, the needs of other provinces, of the whole Society, and of non-Jesuits are to be considered.

211   Major superiors can require that individual communities, according to their capacities, contribute a certain sum of money to the relief of the needs of other communities or apostolic institutes of the province or of the region even if this should require some reduction in their standard of living, which in any case must always be frugal.

212   With due respect for the needs of apostolic institutes and, if this applies, for the statutes of the institute and the will of benefactors, provincials, with the approval of the general, will provide for a more equitable and apostolically effective sharing of resources among the apostolic institutes of the province, looking always to God's greater service.

213   §1. A Charitable and Apostolic Fund of the Society is to be established for the benefit of communities and works of the Society and, should need arise, for externs as well. Money received is not to be permanently invested.

§2. Father General is to determine the sources of this fund, its administration, and the manner of distributing its benefits, with the assistance of advisers from different parts of the Society.

214   It is not allowed to collect alms in another province or region without the permission of the respective major superior.

CHAPTER 3

AVOIDING EVERY APPEARANCE OF AVARICE AND COMMERCE

215   §1. We must carefully avoid even the appearance of engaging in commerce or of seeking profit.

§2. In the Society the general is the competent authority to permit any commercial activity that is necessary or useful for the apostolate, for example, a printing press.

WEEK X, DAY 1

This week we will contemplate the last section of Part VI of the Constitutions, which takes up various topics of our spiritual and apostolic life. This section of the Complementary Norms can serve as an introduction to this contemplation and examination of consciousness.

Preparation for Prayer: see p. 3 of this volume.

What do I desire? That God give me (us) a profound appreciation and love of our way of life.

Other Matters Concerning Our Way of Life:
The Spiritual Life of Our Formed Members
Complementary Norms, Part VI, Section 5, Chapter 1

223   §1. Since the goal to which the Society rightly aspires is "to aid its own members and their fellow men and women to attain the ultimate end for which they were created," "what might be called, in contemporary terms, the total and integral liberation of man, leading to participation in the life of God himself," our life must be undividedly apostolic and religious. This intimate connection between religious and apostolic aspects ought to animate our whole way of living, praying, and working in the Society and to impress on it an apostolic character.

§2. The service of faith and the promotion of justice must be the integrating factor of our inner life as individuals, as communities, and as a worldwide brotherhood.

§3. Hence, all Ours are urged to strive each day, personally and communally, toward an even greater integration of our spiritual life and apostolate, by which they will find God in all things, the God who is present in this world, in its struggle between good and evil, between faith and unbelief, between the yearning for justice and peace and the growing reality of injustice and strife. We should also seek to be enriched in our own spirituality by the spiritual experiences and ethical values, theological perspectives, and symbolic expressions of other religions.

§4. If we are thus to hear and respond to the call of God in this kind of world, we must have a discerning attitude both individually and in community. We cannot attain this discerning attitude without self-abnegation, which is the fruit of our joy at the approach of the Kingdom and results from a progressive identification with Christ.

224   §1. To achieve such integration, it is crucial for us to use all means to foster that familiarity with God in both prayer and action which St. Ignatius considered absolutely essential to the very existence of our companionship. But we cannot achieve this familiarity with God unless we regularly engage in personal prayer.

§2. The Jesuit apostle goes forth from the Exercises, at once a school of prayer and of the apostolate, a man called by his vocation to be a contemplative in action. We must contemplate our world as Ignatius did his, that we may hear anew the call of Christ dying and rising in the anguish and aspirations of men and women.

For Prayer, Reflection, and Discussion

What are my reactions and reflections as I ponder these norms in prayer? Do the norms resonate with my own deepest desires? with my experience? Is the Lord revealing anything to me about my own way of praying? my own trust in God? Are my prayer life and my apostolic life an integrated whole, or at least, moving in that direction? Do I feel called to any change in the way I proceed?

Week X, Day 2

Ignatius is here reflecting on the ideal of the formed Jesuit. He keeps ever in mind the purposes for which the Society of Jesus was founded. He presumes that the formed Jesuit will be a man of prayer, a man who is mortified, a man of prudence. Our most recent congregations have reflected on this same ideal with these purposes in mind and taken into account the changed ecclesiastical circumstances. CN no. 225, §1 presumes, as does Ignatius in the Exercises, that God communicates himself in prayer. We are invited to reflect on our own practices in the light of these texts.

Preparation for Prayer: see p. 3 of this volume.

What do I desire? That God give me (us) a profound appreciation and love of our way of life.

Other Matters Concerning Our Way of Life, *continued*
Constitutions, Part VI

[582]   1. Given the length of time and approbation of their life which are required before admission into the Society among the professed and also the formed coadjutors, it is presupposed that those so admitted will be men who are spiritual and sufficiently advanced that they will run in the path of Christ our Lord to the extent that their bodily strength and the exterior occupations undertaken through charity and obedience allow. Therefore, in what pertains to prayer, meditation, and study, and also in regard to the bodily practices of fasts, vigils, and other austerities or penances, it does not seem proper to give them any other rule than that which discreet charity dictates to them *[A]*, provided that the confessor always be informed and also, when a doubt about advisability arises, the superior [clarified by *CN* no. 225]. Only this will be said in general: On the one hand, they should take care that the excessive use of these practices not weaken their bodily strength or take up so much time that they are rendered incapable of helping the neighbor spiritually according to our Institute; on the other hand, they should be vigilant that these practices not be relaxed to such an extent that the spirit grows cold and the human and lower passions grow warm.

[583]   *A. If the superior thinks it expedient to give some subjects a prescribed time to keep them from exceeding or falling short in their spiritual exercises, he may do so. So too in regard to the use of the other means: if he judges that one ought to be employed without leaving it to the discretion of the individual, he will proceed in accordance with what God our Lord leads him to think proper. And the part of the subject will be to accept with complete devotion the order which is given to him.*

[584]   2. The frequentation of the sacraments should be highly recom
mended; and Holy Communion or the celebration of Mass should not be
postponed beyond eight days without reasons legitimate in the opinion of the
superior [modified by *CN* no. 227].

Complementary Norms, Part VI

225   §1. Therefore, the traditional hour of prayer is to be adapted so
that each Jesuit, guided by his superior, takes into account his particular
circumstances and needs, in the light of that discerning love which St.
Ignatius clearly presupposed in the Constitutions.

§2. All should recall that the prayer in which God communicates
himself more abundantly is the better prayer, whether it is mental or even
vocal, whether it consists in meditative reading or in an intense feeling of
love and self-giving. Prayer thus becomes a truly vital activity whose
progressive growth makes increasingly evident in us the action and
presence of God, whereby we are enabled to seek, love, and serve him in
all things.

§3. Ours are also to give sufficient time to preparation for prayer
and to spiritual reading.

226   §1. The local superior is also responsible for the spiritual vitality
of the community. He should therefore consider it part of his duty to
provide the conditions that foster personal and community prayer, the
sacramental life, and communication on a spiritual level. He should also
take care that every Jesuit finds in the organization of community life
whatever is necessary for recollection and for a suitable balance between
work and rest.

§2. He should also provide at times, in a way that is appropriate
for each apostolic community, a longer period for prayerful interchange as
an opportunity for reflecting before God on the mission of the community
and, at the same time, for expressing the apostolic character of our
prayer.

227   §1. Every community of the Society is a faith community that
comes together in the Eucharist with others who believe in Christ to
celebrate their common faith. More than anything else, our participation
at the same table in the Body and Blood of Christ makes us one companionship totally dedicated to Christ's mission in today's world.

§2. According to the prescriptions of their own rite, all should
take part in the daily celebration of the Eucharist and consider it as the
center of their religious and apostolic lives. Communitarian celebrations of
the Eucharist are encouraged, especially on days when the community
can more easily gather. Moreover, for the faithful fulfillment of their

apostolic vocation, both communities and individuals should cherish daily converse with Christ the Lord in visiting the Blessed Sacrament.

§3. Likewise, so that they might increase in purity of soul and in freedom in God's service, all should also frequently receive the sacrament of reconciliation; they should also willingly participate in community penitential services and strive to promote the spirit of reconciliation in our communities. Each one should have his own fixed confessor to whom he ordinarily confesses.

For Prayer, Reflection, and Discussion

What reactions and reflections do I have as I ponder these texts in prayer? Do my practices correspond with or, at least, move toward the ideals set forth? What desires are raised in me as I ponder these texts? Do I sense that the Lord is calling me to change anything in my prayer and devotional life? What is my experience of liturgy? How do I react to the tradition of daily liturgy that is expected of all Jesuits? Is the Lord revealing anything to us (my community, my province) through my interior reactions in prayer?

WEEK X, DAY 3

Once again we see how Ignatius made very practical decisions about our way of proceeding in order to preserve the Society's freedom to carry out the mission given it by the Lord and his Church. The Complementary Norms interpret for our time some of the stipulations of the Constitutions regarding our work and our prayer. The proscription against taking on the spiritual care of women has been interpreted to mean that Jesuits should not take on the care of various institutes. It does not preclude spiritual direction of individuals.

Preparation for Prayer: see p. 3 of this volume.

What do I desire? That God give me (us) a profound appreciation and love of our way of life.

Other Matters Concerning Our Way of Life, *continued*

Constitutions, Part VI

[586]   4. Because the occupations which are undertaken for the aid of souls are of great importance, proper to our Institute, and very frequent; and because, on the other hand, our residence in one place or another is so uncertain, they will not regularly hold choir for the canonical hours or sing Masses and offices. For those whose devotion urges them to hear such will have no lack of places to satisfy themselves, and our members ought to apply their efforts to the pursuits that are most proper to our vocation, for the glory of God our Lord.

[588]   5. Likewise, because the members of this Society ought to be ready at any hour to go to any part of the world where they may be sent by the sovereign pontiff or their own superiors, they ought not to take on the care of souls [clarified by *CN* no. 274, with regard to taking on parishes], and still less ought they to take charge of religious women or any other women whatever to be their regular confessors or to direct them [modified by *CN* no. 237]. However, nothing prohibits them on a single occasion from hearing the confessions of a whole monastery for special reasons.

[589]   6. Neither should the members take on obligations of Masses which are to be celebrated perpetually in their churches, or similar burdens which are incompatible with the freedom required for our manner of proceeding in the Lord.

Complementary Norms, Part VI

228   In the recitation of the Liturgy of the Hours, to which they are obligated by the reception of ordination, our priests and deacons should try to pray attentively and at the appropriate time that wonderful song of praise which is truly the prayer of Christ to the Father, in union with his Body.

229   Twice daily the examination of conscience should be made, which, in accord with Ignatius's intent, contributes so much to discernment regarding our entire apostolic life, to purity of heart, and to familiarity with God in the midst of an active life. In accord with the approved tradition of the Society, it is recommended that it last a quarter of an hour.

230   Insofar as their apostolic character permits, Jesuit communities should come together daily for some brief common prayer.

231   §1. Because it is especially in the Spiritual Exercises that we experience Christ and respond to him calling us to the Society, they are the source and center of our vocation and an altogether special means

both for fostering renewal and union in the Society and for carrying on our apostolic mission in a more profound way. Hence, they should be made for eight successive days each year; certain adaptations may be allowed, of which the provincial is to be the judge.

§2. In addition, it is recommended that

1° Especially at the time of the annual visitation, the provincials inquire about the way our members are making the Spiritual Exercises

2° Those who are already formed be encouraged to make the full Exercises even extended over a month

3° In the provinces the greatest care be given to the formation of those who have the talent to direct the Exercises

4° Those already formed should at times make the annual retreat under the personal direction of a skilled director

232   Since dialogue with a spiritual director on a regular basis is a great help for growing in spiritual insight and learning discernment, all of Ours, even when engaged in an active apostolate, should highly esteem spiritual direction and should openly and frequently speak with a spiritual director.

233   We should make the love of Christ, symbolized in the devotion to the Sacred Heart of Jesus, the center of our own spiritual lives, so as more effectively to proclaim before all people the unfathomable riches of Christ and to foster the primacy of love in Christian life.

234   All of Ours should consider, as something most earnestly recommended to them, devotion to the Blessed Virgin Mary, whom our Society has always honored as a mother.

237   Our members may not undertake the care of institutes of consecrated life, societies of apostolic life, or similar associations; consequently, they are forbidden to govern them or to involve themselves in their concerns.

For Prayer, Reflection, and Discussion

What reactions and reflections do I have as I ponder these texts in prayer? Do I make choices in my life based on Ignatian criteria? Do I engage in the daily examination of conscience so prized by Ignatius? Have I experienced the examination of conscience as a way to achieve some of the purposes foreseen in *CN* no. 229? Is the Lord revealing anything to me (us) through my reactions and reflections?

Week X, Day 4

Jesuit formation is a never ending phenomenon, precisely because we are on a pathway to God, the ever greater One whom we can neither fathom nor possess, but who can deepen his possession of us, his servants.

Preparation for Prayer: see p. 3 of this volume.

What do I desire? That God give me (us) a profound appreciation and love of our way of life.

Other Matters Concerning Our Way of Life, *continued*
Spiritual Progress and Ongoing Formation
Complementary Norms, Part VI

240   Especially in our times a truly contemporary apostolate demands of us a process of permanent and continuing formation. Thus formation is never ended, and our "first" formation must be seen as the beginning of this continuing process.

241   All, even those who have already completed their formation, should strive constantly to nourish and renew their own spiritual lives from those sources that the Church and the Society give us (biblical study, theological reflection, liturgy, Spiritual Exercises, recollections, spiritual reading, and the like). Thus, with the advance of years, each one should experience constant rejuvenation in his spiritual life, and his apostolic activity should increasingly become able to respond more effectively to the needs of the Church and of men and women.

242   §1. Ours achieve continuing formation especially through a constant evaluation of and reflection on their apostolate, in the light of faith and with the help of their apostolic community. Our professors and experts should also assist in this, shedding the light of their theories on our praxis, even while they themselves are led to more profound reflection by the apostolic experience of their companions.

§2. This continuing formation demands that definite periods of time be given to formal courses or simply to private study, whether in theology or other disciplines, as required for one's apostolate. As far as foreign languages are concerned, insofar as possible our formed members are encouraged to follow what is prescribed in no. 97 for those in formation.

§3. Continuing formation should also foster an attitude of universalism by providing an opportunity for members to experience the international character of the Society.

243   §1. In accord with the resources and the apostolic needs of the different provinces and regions, major superiors should provide for the

spiritual, intellectual, and apostolic renewal of all our members. At determined times let Ours be given sufficient opportunity to apply themselves
seriously to this sort of renewal according to a program to be approved
by the major superiors.

§2. An appropriate course or program on spiritual and doctrinal
formation should also be set up each year for the brothers, especially for
those who have not yet completed their final probation. On such occasions, lectures are to be offered on Sacred Scripture, liturgy, theology,
and social doctrine.

§3. It is suggested that our members, priests and brothers alike,
after completing about ten years in apostolic ministries and offices, be
given the opportunity for more intensive spiritual, psychological, and
apostolic renewal during a period of at least three months.

For Prayer, Reflection, and Discussion

What reactions and reflections do I have as I ponder these texts in
prayer? What has been my experience of continuing formation? Does
reflection on these texts raise any questions about my practice of
continuing formation? about the practice of my community or
province?

WEEK X, DAY 5

*In the Principle and Foundation Ignatius says: "Consequently, on our own
part we ought not to seek health rather than sickness, wealth rather than
poverty, honor rather than dishonor, a long life rather than a short one, and
so on in all other matters. Rather, we ought to desire and choose only that
which is more conducive to the end for which we are created." As he finishes
this part of the Constitutions devoted to the way of life of the formed Jesuit,
Ignatius points out that even in his dying the Jesuit should be living out his
vocation.*

Preparation for Prayer: see p. 3 of this volume.

What do I desire? That God give me (us) a profound appreciation and love of our way of life.

Other Matters Concerning Our Way of Life, *continued*
The Help Given to the Dying Members of the Society

Constitutions, Part VI

[595]   1. As during his whole life, so also and even more at the time of his death, each member of the Society ought to strive earnestly that through him God our Lord may be glorified and served and his neighbors may be edified, at least by the example of his patience and fortitude along with his living faith, hope, and love of the eternal goods which Christ our Lord merited and acquired for us by those altogether incomparable sufferings of his temporal life and death. But sickness is often such that it greatly impairs the use of the mental faculties; and through the vehement attacks of the devil and the great importance of not succumbing to him, the passing away is itself such that the sick man needs help from fraternal charity. Therefore with great vigilance the superior should see to it that the one who in the physician's opinion is in danger should, before being deprived of his judgment, receive all the holy sacraments and fortify himself for the passage from this temporal life to that which is eternal, by means of the arms which the divine liberality of Christ our Lord offers.

[596]   2. He ought likewise to be aided by the very special prayers of all the members of the community, until he has given up his soul to his Creator. Besides others who may come in to witness the sick man's death, in greater or lesser number as the superior judges, some ought to be especially assigned to keep him company. They should encourage him and afford him the reminders and helps which are appropriate at that moment. When in time he can no longer be helped, they should commend him to God our Lord, until his soul now freed from the body is received by him who redeemed it by that price so high, his blood and life.

Complementary Norms, Part VI

244   §1. Our elderly and infirm members continue to be apostolically fruitful and make others sharers in their own wisdom, acquired by the experience of serving our mission. They ought to take care that others are encouraged by the example of their filial and confident dedication to God in sickness and failing strength.

§2. We should all have a special spiritual and human care for them, with profound gratitude and fraternal charity. Superiors have a special responsibility to do this.

§3. Major superiors should give to our elderly and infirm members a special mission to pray for the Church and the Society and to unite their personal suffering and limitations to the worldwide salvific ministry of the Church and the Society.

§4. In the light of present-day progress in medical science and, in particular, the possibility on the one hand of prolonging human life beyond its normal natural limits and on the other hand of helping others in certain circumstances by donating one's own bodily organs, each one should determine—according to the laws of each region—what in conscience he considers to be the better expression, the one enlightened by faith in Jesus Christ, of his own personal dignity and a sense of solidarity with others, at the moment of his transition from earthly to eternal life in the Lord.

For Prayer, Reflection, and Discussion

What reactions and reflections do I have as I ponder these texts in prayer? Do I, at least occasionally, reflect on sickness and dying? Do I care for my sick and dying brothers in the manner Ignatius recommends? Am I satisfied with the way the community and the province take care of the sick and dying? Is the Lord revealing anything to us through my reactions to these texts?

WEEK X, DAY 6

Here we have a characteristic of Ignatian governance. Ignatius wanted the sweet law of love to be the motive for our observation of the Constitutions. Prayerful reflection on this text will serve as a fitting entrée to this day of recapitulation. With this week we finish our prayer and reflection on Part VI of the Constitutions, on the personal life of Jesuits.

Preparation for Prayer: see p. 3 of this volume.

What do I desire? That God give me (us) a profound appreciation and love of our way of life.

Recapitulation
The Constitutions Do Not Oblige under Pain of Sin
Constitutions, Part VI, Chapter 5

[602]   The Society desires that all the Constitutions and Declarations and its regime of living should be observed in every regard according to our Institute, without deviation in anything; and on the other hand it also desires that its individual members may be safe, or aided against falling into any occasion of sin which could arise on account of the said Constitutions or ordinances. For that reason it is our considered opinion in our Lord that, apart from the express vow which the Society has with respect to the currently reigning sovereign pontiff, and apart from the other three essential vows of poverty, chastity, and obedience, no constitutions, declarations, or regime of living can oblige under mortal or venial sin, unless the superior orders the subjects in the name of Christ our Lord or in virtue of obedience, which may be done in regard to things and persons where it is judged to be highly expedient for the particular good of each one or for the universal good. Thus the fear of sin should give place to the love and desire of all perfection and of contributing to the greater glory and praise of Christ our Creator and Lord.

For Prayer, Reflection, and Discussion

As I reflect on my reactions during the past week, what stands out? What do I want to share with my group? What is the Lord revealing to us about our way of life?

WEEK XI, DAY 1

Part VII takes up the choice of ministries and the criteria by which the Society makes such choices. The text of the Complementary Norms presented here comes from our latest congregations and contains the Society's discernment of its mission today.

Preparation for Prayer: see p. 3 of this volume.

What do I desire? That God give me (us) a profound appreciation and love of our mission.

Our Mission and Criteria for Choosing Ministry

The Relations to Their Neighbor of Those Already Incorporated into the Society When They Are Dispersed into the Vineyard of Christ Our Lord

Constitutions, Part VII

The Mission of the Society Today

Complementary Norms, Part VII

245   §1. The mission of the Society today is participation in the total evangelizing mission of the Church, which aims at the realization of the Kingdom of God in the whole of human society, not only in the life to come but also in this life. This mission is "a single but complex reality, which is expressed in a variety of ways"; namely, through the interrelated dimensions of the witness of one's life; of proclamation, conversion, inculturation, and of the establishment of local churches; and also through dialogue and the promotion of the justice desired by God.

§2. Within this framework and in accordance with our original charism approved by the Church, the contemporary mission of the Society is the service of faith and the promotion in society of that justice of the Gospel that is the embodiment of God's love and saving mercy.

§3. In this mission, its aim (the service of faith) and its integrating principle (faith directed toward the justice of the Kingdom) are dynamically related to the inculturated proclamation of the Gospel and to dialogue with other religious traditions as integral dimensions of evangelization.

246   Conditions for carrying out this mission are the following:

1° A continuing personal conversion, finding Jesus Christ in the brokenness of our world, living in solidarity with the poor and outcast, so that we can take up their cause under the standard of the cross. Our sensitivity to such a mission will be most affected by frequent direct contact with these "friends of the Lord," from whom we can often learn much about faith. Some insertion into the world of the poor should therefore be part of the life of each member, and our communities should be located among ordinary people wherever possible.

2° A dialogue, born of respect for people, especially the poor, in which we share their cultural and spiritual values and offer our own cultural and spiritual resources, in order to build up a communion of peoples instructed by God's Word and enlivened by the Spirit as at

Pentecost. In such a dialogue, we come into contact with the activity of God in the lives of other men and women, and we try to enable people to become aware of God's presence in their culture. This dialogue is also necessary in the so-called "post-Christian" cultures, based upon a sharing of life, a shared commitment to action for human development and liberation, a sharing of values and a sharing of human experience.

3° A deep respect for everything that has been brought about in human beings by the Spirit who blows where he wills; attention to the global desire for a contemplative experience of the divine; a desire to be enriched by the spiritual experiences and ethical values, theological perspectives, and symbolic expressions of other religions.

4° A desire to embody Christ's ministry of healing and reconciliation in a world increasingly divided by economic and social status, race and ethnicity, violence and war, cultural and religious pluralism.

5° A closer collaboration with others, especially with the laity, with other members of local churches, with Christians of other denominations, with adherents to other religions, and all "who hunger and thirst after justice"; in short, with all who strive to make a world fit for men and women to live in, a world where the brotherhood of all opens the way for the recognition and acceptance of Christ Jesus and God our Father.

6° A more profound spiritual experience through the Spiritual Exercises, by which we continually renew our faith and apostolic hope by experiencing again the love of God in Christ Jesus. We strengthen our commitment to be "companions of Jesus" in his mission, to labor with him in solidarity with the poor for the establishment of the Kingdom.

7° All the major problems of our time have an international dimension. On our part, great solidarity and availability and real openness to change will be necessary, even as we remain firmly rooted in our own culture, in order to foster the growth of cooperation and coordination throughout the whole Society, in the service of the worldwide mission of the Church.

8° We must therefore have an operative freedom: open, adaptable, even eager for any mission that may be given us. Our desire is an unconditional consecration to mission, free of all worldly interest and free to serve all men and women. Our mission extends to the creation of this same spirit of mission in others.

WEEK XI, DAY 2

The text of the Complementary Norms presented here reflects the decrees of GC 34 which expanded on decree 4 of GC 32.

Preparation for Prayer: see p. 3 of this volume.

What do I desire? That God give me (us) a profound appreciation and love of our mission.

Our Mission and Criteria for Choosing Ministry, *continued*
Complementary Norms, Part VII

247　§1. As far as the promotion of justice is concerned, we must become more aware, as the Church itself has done, of its more recent and new exigencies for our mission; such are, among others, protection of the human rights of persons and peoples (individual, socioeconomic, civil and political, the right to peace, to progress, to cultural integrity); the disturbing consequences of the interdependence of peoples, causing grave damage to the quality of life and culture of poor peoples, especially of "indigenous" peoples; safeguarding human life itself, from its beginning to its natural end, life that is severely threatened by the so-called "culture of death"; the influence of the media in the service of justice, which requires coordinated action of Christians and other persons in different areas; protection of the environment; the tragic marginalization of not a few nations, especially on the African continent at this time; the need of the peoples of Eastern Europe to find a sure way to a future in freedom, peace, and security; the problem of the socially marginalized in every society; the very grave worldwide situation of refugees.

§2. The situation of women in the world today merits special attention. Our contribution to overcoming unjust structures and experiencing our solidarity with women include the following: teaching the essential equality of women and men; supporting women in opposing situations of exploitation and violence; fostering an appropriate presence of women in our ministries and institutions and involving women in decision making in our ministries; promoting the education of women and elimination of all forms of discrimination in it; using appropriately inclusive language in speaking and writing.

§3. All these efforts must be concentrated on transforming the cultural values that sustain an unjust and oppressive social order.

248   Father General, with the help of his council, has the task of stimulating the entire Society to serve the cause of the Gospel and its justice. But all our members, especially major superiors, should strenuously collaborate with him, even if this might shake up their settled habits or even disturb their peace of mind, when they are accustomed instead to work of a less universal scope.

249   §1. Any realistic desire to engage in the promotion of justice in our mission will mean some kind of involvement in civic activity; but this will make our preaching of the Gospel more meaningful and its acceptance easier.

§2. Communities and superiors should help each one of us to overcome the difficulties, fear, and apathy that block us from truly comprehending the cultural, social, economic, and political problems existing in our city, country, or region, as well as in the world at large. In this way let each identify and assume the responsibilities to society that are his, and let each in his own proper way participate in the efforts needed to promote genuine justice.

§3. In each of our different apostolates, we must create communities of solidarity in seeking justice. Working together with our colleagues, we can and should engage in every ministry of the Society to promote justice in one or more of the following ways: directly serving and accompanying the poor, developing awareness of the demands of justice joined to the social responsibility to achieve it, and participating in social mobilization for the creation of a more just social order.

250   All our members, but especially those who belong to the affluent world, should endeavor to work as much as is appropriate with those who form public opinion, as well as with international organizations, to promote justice more effectively among all peoples.

251   Finally, in carrying out this mission of ours with exactitude, we should ever keep in mind that "the means which unite the human instrument to God and so dispose it that it may be wielded dexterously by his divine hand are more effective than those which equip it in relation to men."

For Prayer, Reflection, and Discussion

What reactions and reflections do I have as I ponder these texts in prayer? Do I feel challenged? Encouraged? Through my reactions is the Lord revealing to me how he views my (our) way of carrying out our mission?

WEEK XI, DAY 3

Ignatius here gives the motivation for the vow of obedience to the pope for mission. The bottom line seems to have been that Ignatius and the first companions wanted to be available for mission and to remove any chance of disordered affection governing the choice of mission. They put their trust in the Lord and in the papacy, as the Lord's privileged instrument of revealing his will for the universal Church. Once again we see Ignatius's mystical vision of obedience in operation.

Preparation for Prayer: see p. 3 of this volume.

What do I desire? That God give me (us) a profound appreciation and love of our mission.

Our Mission and Criteria for Choosing Ministry, *continued*
Missions from the Supreme Pontiff
Constitutions, Part VII

[603]   1. Just as Part VI treats of what each member of the Society needs to observe in regard to himself, so this Part VII deals with what the members need to observe in regard to their neighbor (which is an end eminently charac-

teristic of our Institute) when they are dispersed throughout Christ's vineyard to labor in that part of it and in that work which have been entrusted to them, whether they have been sent to some places or others by either the supreme vicar of Christ our Lord or the superiors of the Society, who for them are similarly in the place of his Divine Majesty; or whether they themselves choose where and in what work they will labor, having been commissioned to travel to any place where they judge that greater service of God and the good of souls will follow; or whether they carry on their labor not by traveling but by residing steadily and continually in certain places where much fruit of glory and service to God is expected [A].

And to treat the missions from His Holiness first as being most important, it should be observed that the vow which the Society made to obey him as the supreme vicar of Christ without any excuse meant that the members were to go to any place where he judges it expedient to send them for the greater glory of God and the good of souls, whether among the faithful or unbelievers [B]. The Society did not mean the vow for a particular place, but rather for being dispersed to various regions and places throughout the world, wishing to make the best choice in this matter by having the sovereign pontiff make the distribution of its members.

[604]   *A. These are the four more general ways of distribution into the vineyard of Christ our Lord. Each of them is treated in its own chapter in this Part VII.*

[605]   *B. The intention of the fourth vow pertaining to the pope was not for a particular place but for having the members dispersed throughout the various parts of the world. For those who first united to form the Society were from different provinces and realms and did not know into which regions they were to go, whether among the faithful or the unbelievers; and therefore, to avoid erring in the path of the Lord, they made the promise or vow in order that His Holiness might distribute them for the greater glory of God, in conformity with their intention to travel throughout the world and, when they could not find the desired spiritual fruit in one place, to pass on to another and another, ever seeking the greater glory of God our Lord and the greater aid of souls.*

[606]   2. In this matter, the Society having placed its own judgment and will wholly under that of Christ our Lord and his vicar, neither the superior for himself nor any individual member of the Society will be permitted to arrange for himself or for another, or to try to arrange, directly or indirectly, with the pope or his ministers to reside in or to be sent rather to one place than another. The individual members will leave this entire concern to the supreme vicar of Christ and to their own superior; and in regard to his own person the superior will in our Lord leave this concern to His Holiness and to the Society.

Missions from the Supreme Pontiff
Complementary Norms, Part VII

252 §1. To be truly Christian, our service to the Church must be anchored in fidelity to Christ, who makes all things new; to be proper to the Society, it must be done in union with the successor of Peter.

§2. Out of love for Christ and in virtue of the fourth vow of special obedience to his vicar concerning missions, the Society offers itself completely to the Church, so that the supreme pontiff may send all its members into the vineyard of the Lord to carry out his mission.

§3. Missions that the supreme pontiff may wish to entrust to our Society at any time and in any part of the world in fulfillment of our mission, we must place in the category of the highest priority of our apostolic activity.

253 The calls that have come to the Society from recent popes are the following:

1° To contribute effectively to the implementation of the Second Vatican Council

2° To confront with all our forces the problem of atheism and cooperate in that profound renewal of the Church needed in a secularized age

3° To better adapt our traditional apostolates to the different spiritual necessities of today: the renewal of Christian life, the education of youth, the formation of the clergy, the study of philosophy and theology, research into humanistic and scientific cultures, and missionary evangelization

4° To pay particular attention to ecumenism, interreligious dialogue, and the task of authentic inculturation

5° In a manner consonant with our priestly and religious Institute and within the Church's evangelizing action, to promote the justice "connected with peace, which is the aspiration of all peoples"

6° To foster the vigorous impulse toward missionary work and church union and to serve our prophetic mission to promote the new evangelization

254 The pontifical mandate entrusted to the Society of resisting atheism should permeate all the accepted forms of our apostolate, in such wise that we may both cultivate among believers true faith and an authentic awareness of God and also zealously direct our efforts to nonbelievers of every type.

WEEK XI, DAY 4

Once again we see the centrality of obedience for Ignatius. Obedience is our way to know the will of God. Ignatius also stresses the need to look to the greater service of God and the universal good. In making his choices the superior general needs to have a "thoroughly right and pure intention in the presence of God our Lord." The text of the Complementary Norms cited here makes it clear that we join the Society, not a province. Hence, just as each professed Jesuit must be ready to heed a mission from the pope, so too each Jesuit must be ready to heed a mission from Father General.

Preparation for Prayer: see p. 3 of this volume.

What do I desire? That God give me (us) a profound appreciation and love of our mission.

Our Mission and Criteria for Choosing Ministry, *continued*
The Missions Received from the Superior of the Society
Constitutions, Part VII

[618]   1. The more readily to be able to meet the spiritual needs of souls in many regions, as also with greater security for those who go for this purpose *[A]*, the superiors of the Society, in accord with the faculty granted by the sovereign pontiff, will have authority to send any of the Society's members *[B]* to whatsoever place these superiors think it more expedient to send them *[C]*, although these members, wherever they are, will always be at the disposition of His Holiness.

Now there are many who make requests more with a view to their own spiritual obligations to their flocks, or to other less immediate advantages, rather than to those that are common or universal. Hence, the superior general, or whoever holds this authority from him, ought to bestow much careful thought on missions of this kind, so that, in sending subjects to one region rather than to another, or for one purpose rather than for another, or one particular person rather than another or several of them, in this manner or in that, or for a longer or shorter time, that may always be done which is conducive to the greater service of God and the universal good.

With this thoroughly right and pure intention in the presence of God our Lord, and—should he think it advisable because of the difficulty or importance of the decision—commending the matter to his Divine Majesty and causing it to be commended in the prayers and Masses of the house, as well as discussing it with one or more members of the Society who happen to be present and whom he thinks suitable, the superior will on his own authority decide about sending or not sending, and about the other circumstances, as he will judge to be expedient for the greater glory of God.

The part of the one who is sent will be, without interposing himself in favor of going or remaining in one place rather than another, to leave the disposition of himself completely and very freely to the superior who in the place of Christ our Lord directs him in the path of his greater service and praise *[I]*. In similar manner, too, no one ought to try by any means to bring it about that others will remain in one place or go to another, unless he does so with the approval of his superior, by whom he should be governed in our Lord.

[619]   *A. The superior of the Society can more easily and more expeditiously make provision for many places (especially those remote from the Apostolic See) than would be the case if those who need members of the Society must always approach the sovereign pontiff. For the individual members, too, there is greater security in going under obedience to their superiors rather than on their own initiative, even supposing they could act in this way and not as sent by the one charged with directing them in the place of Christ our Lord, as the interpreter of his divine will.*

[620]   *B. Just as the general can perform the other functions by himself and through persons under him, so too can he perform this one of sending his subjects on missions, by reserving to himself the missions which he thinks should be thus reserved.*

[621]   *C. The sending of subjects "to whatsoever place these superiors think it expedient" means either among the faithful, even though it be in the Indies, or among the unbelievers, especially where there is a community of believers, as in Greece and elsewhere. Where the inhabitants are more exclusively unbelievers, the superior should ponder seriously in the sight of God our Lord whether he ought to*

send subjects or not, and where, and whom. The part of the subject will always be to accept his mission joyfully as coming from God our Lord.

[627]   *I. This prescription is not violated if someone represents the motions or thoughts that occur to him contrary to an order received, meanwhile submitting his entire judgment and will to the judgment and will of his superior, who is in the place of Christ our Lord.*

Complementary Norms, Part VII

255   §1. All members of the Society of Jesus, even though dispersed in various local communities and ascribed to individual provinces and regions, are inserted directly and primarily into the single apostolic body and community of the whole Society. It is at this level that the overall apostolic decisions and guidelines are worked out and established, for which each one should feel responsible. This demands of all of us a high degree of availability and a real apostolic mobility in the service of the universal Church.

§2. This solidarity with the body of the Society ought to take precedence over any other loyalties (those binding a man to any type of institution, within or outside the Society). It ought to mark any other commitment, transforming it thereby into a "mission." For a "mission" as such is bestowed by the Society through the superior and is always subject to its review. The Society can confirm or modify it as the greater service of God may require.

For Prayer, Reflection, and Discussion

What reactions and reflections do I have as I ponder these texts in prayer? Has our province taken on a mission at the behest of Father General? If so, how have such missions affected us? What is the Lord revealing to me (us) through my reactions to these texts?

These are the criteria given to Father General by Ignatius for the choice of ministries. They should ground all our apostolic choices.

Preparation for Prayer: see p. 3 of this volume.

What do I desire? That God give me (us) a profound appreciation and love of our mission.

Our Mission and Criteria for Choosing Ministry, *continued*
Constitutions, Part VII

[622]   *D. To make the best choice in sending persons to one place or another while having the greater service of God and the more universal good before one's eyes as the guiding norm, it would appear that in the ample vineyard of the Lord one ought to select, other things being equal (and this should be understood in everything that follows), that part of the vineyard which has greater need, both because of lack of other workers, and because of the wretchedness and infirmity of the people there and their danger of eternal condemnation.*

Consideration should also be given to where greater fruit is likely to be reaped through the means usual in the Society; as would be the case where one sees the door more widely open and a better disposition and readiness among the people to be profited. This would consist in their greater devotion and desire (which can be judged in part by the insistence they show), or in the condition and quality of the persons who are more capable of making progress and of preserving the fruit produced, to the glory of God our Lord.

In places where our indebtedness is greater, for example, where there is a house or college of the Society, or members of it engaged in study, who are recipients of charitable deeds from the people there, and assuming that the other considerations pertaining to spiritual progress are equal, it would be more suitable to have some laborers there, preferring these places to others for these considerations in conformity with perfect charity.

The more universal the good is, the more is it divine. Hence preference ought to be given to persons and places which, once benefited themselves, are a cause of extending the good to many others who are under their influence or take guidance from them.

For that reason, the spiritual aid which is given to important and public persons ought to be regarded as more important, since it is a more universal good. This is true (whether these persons are laymen such as princes, lords, magistrates, or administrators of justice, or whether they are clerics such as prelates). This holds true also of spiritual aid given to persons who are distinguished for learning and authority, for the same reason of the good being more universal. For that same reason, too, preference ought to be shown to the aid which is given to large nations such as the Indies, or to important cities, or to universities, which are generally attended by numerous persons who, if aided themselves, can become laborers for the help of others.

Similarly, in places where the enemy of Christ our Lord is seen to have sown cockle [Matt. 13:24–30], particularly where he has spread bad opinion about the Society or stirred up ill will against it so as to impede the fruit which it might produce, the Society ought to exert itself more, especially if it is an important place of which account should be taken; persons should be sent there, if possible, who by their life and learning may undo the evil opinion founded on false reports.

[623]   *E. For making a better choice of the undertakings on which the superior sends his men, the same rule should be kept in view, namely, that of considering the greater divine honor and the greater universal good. This consideration can quite legitimately suggest sending persons to one place rather than to another.*

To touch upon some motives which can exist in favor of one place rather than another, we mention these:

First of all, where members of the Society have the possibility of engaging in works aimed at spiritual benefits and also in works aimed at corporal benefits where mercy and charity are exercised; or of helping persons in matters of greater perfection and also of lesser perfection; and, in fine, in things which are in themselves more good and also less good—then, if both things cannot be done simultaneously (everything else being equal), the first ought always to be preferred to the second.

Likewise, when there are matters in the service of God our Lord which are more urgent, and others which are less pressing and can better suffer postponement of the remedy, even if they are of equal importance, the first should be preferred to the second.

Similarly too, when there are matters that are especially incumbent upon the Society, or clearly without anyone else to attend to them, and others for which other persons do have a care and means of providing, the first kind should rightly be preferred to the second in selecting missions.

Likewise, among pious works of equal importance, urgency, and need, when some are safer for those engaged in them and others more dangerous, and when some are dispatched more easily and quickly, whereas others are more difficult and take longer time, the first should be similarly preferred to the second.

All things mentioned above being equal, when there are occupations which are of more universal good and extend to the aid of greater numbers of our neighbors, such as preaching or lecturing, and others aimed more at individuals, such as hearing confessions or giving the Exercises, and it is impossible to accomplish both at once, then preference should be given to the first, unless there should be circumstances through which it would be judged that it would be more expedient to take up the second.

Similarly too, when there are pious works that continue longer and are permanently profitable, such as are certain pious foundations for the aid of our neighbors, and others that are less durable and give help only on a few occasions and for a short time, then it is certain that the first ought to be preferred to the second. Hence the superior of the Society ought to employ his subjects more in the first than in the second, always as being for the greater divine service and greater good for our neighbors.

For Prayer, Reflection, and Discussion

What reactions and reflections do I have as I ponder these texts in prayer? It might be profitable to make an examination of consciousness regarding my own choice of apostolic ministry. Have I followed the criteria outlined by Ignatius? Does the community or province seem to have followed these criteria in choosing ministries? Is the Lord revealing anything to me (us) through my reactions and reflections?

WEEK XI, DAY 6

These texts from the Complementary Norms can serve as a way to recapitulate the reflections of this week. They ask the Society to evaluate our present choice of ministries and how we engage in these ministries in the light of the criteria of the Constitutions and of the conditions of the modern world.

Preparation for Prayer: see p. 3 of this volume.

What do I desire? That God give me (us) a profound appreciation and love of our mission.

Our Mission and Criteria for Choosing Ministry, *continued*
Complementary Norms, Part VII

256   §1. As we continue to respond to our mission today as it is described by recent general congregations, traditional apostolates, appropriately updated, take on fresh importance, while new needs and situations make new demands on us, so that all our works may contribute to strengthening the faith that does justice.

§2. Hence all our ministries, both traditional and new, must be reviewed by means of apostolic spiritual discernment, both personal and communitarian, with great attention to the role they can play in the service of faith and the promotion of justice, in solidarity with the poor, so that, if need be, they may be replaced by others which are more effective.

257   Our institutions can use the following means to help them implement our mission more effectively: institutional evaluation of the role they play in society; discernment whether the institution's own internal structures and policies reflect our mission; collaboration and exchange with similar institutions in diverse social and cultural contexts; continuing formation of personnel regarding mission.

258   §1. All our members, especially superiors, to whom the choice of ministries belongs "as the most important task of all," must make great efforts to bring about this review of our ministries. The criteria for review, found in the Constitutions themselves and illuminated by the decrees of the general congregations and the instructions of the superiors general, retain their perennial validity, but none the less must always be rightly applied to historical circumstances.

§2. We should always keep in mind social conditions and pastoral programs, the apostolic forces available or hoped for, the more pressing pastoral and apostolic needs, and the help that ought to be given to Father General for more universal works.

§3. Social and cultural analysis of the true state of affairs should also be employed from a religious, social, and political point of view, based on serious and specialized studies and on an accurate knowledge of those matters.

§4. According to this way of proceeding, which is to be used by local, provincial, and regional communities, superiors can employ the customary consultations and then draw up apostolic options to be submitted to Father General.

For Prayer, Reflection, and Discussion

As I ponder these texts and reflect on the past week, what stands out for me? What were my strong reactions, both positive and negative? Is the Lord revealing anything to me (us) by my reactions and reflections and the discussions in our group?

Week XII, Day 1

Here we see the practical wisdom of Ignatius to try, as far as possible, to achieve an efficacious mission. Prudence is central to the mission spirituality of the Society.

Preparation for Prayer: see p. 3 of this volume.

What do I desire? That God give me (us) a profound appreciation and love of our mission.

Our Mission and Criteria for Choosing Ministry, *continued*
Constitutions, Part VII

[624]   *F. Although it is the supreme providence and direction of the Holy Spirit that must efficaciously bring us to make the right decision in all matters, and to send to each place those who are best fitted and suited to the people and tasks for which they are sent, still this much may be said in general. First, that for matters of greater moment and where it is more important to avoid mistakes, so far as this depends on the one who with God's grace is to provide, persons ought to be sent who are more select and in whom greater confidence is had.*

In matters that involve greater bodily labors, persons more strong and healthy.

In matters which contain greater spiritual dangers, persons more proven in virtue and more reliable.

To go to astute persons who hold posts of spiritual or temporal government, those members seem most suitable who excel in discretion and grace of conversation, and who (while not lacking interior qualities) have an outward appearance which may enhance their authority; for their counsel can be of great moment.

To deal with persons of subtle intelligence and learning, those are more suitable who are especially gifted with intelligence and learning; for these persons can be of more assistance in lectures and conversations.

For the ordinary people, those will generally be most apt who have talent for preaching, hearing confessions, and so on.

The number and combination of laborers to be sent should also receive consideration. First of all, it would be wise when possible not to send one person by himself, but instead at least two persons, so that they may be of greater aid to one another in spiritual and bodily matters, and also, by dividing up among themselves the labors in the service of their neighbor, be of more benefit to those to whom they are sent.

Moreover, if two are to go, it seems that a preacher or lecturer could well be accompanied by someone who through confessions and spiritual exercises could gather in the harvest which the other prepares for him, and could assist him by conversations and the other means used in dealing with our neighbors.

Likewise, when a person is sent who is less experienced in the Society's manner of proceeding and of dealing with the neighbor, it seems that he ought to be accompanied by another who has more experience therein, whom he can imitate, consult, and get advice from in matters where he is uncertain.

With a person who is very ardent and daring it seems that there could well go another who is more circumspect and cautious. The like holds for other combinations of this kind, in such a way that their difference, united by the bond of charity, may be helpful to both and not be able to engender contradiction or discord between the two of them or with their neighbors.

To send more than two when the importance of the work intended in the service of God our Lord is greater and requires a larger number, and when the Society can provide more laborers without prejudice to other things conducive to the greater divine glory and universal good, is something which the superior will have authority to do, accordingly as the unction of the Holy Spirit inspires him or as he judges in the sight of his Divine Majesty to be better and more expedient.

[625]   G. In regard to the manner in which he is to send them (after the proper instruction), the superior should deliberate whether he will send them in the manner of the poor, so that they would go on foot and without money, or with better facilities; whether with or without letters to aid toward winning acceptance and benevolence at their destination; and whether these letters should be addressed to individuals, or the city, or its head. In regard to all the details, the superior will consider the greater edification of the neighbor and the service of God our Lord and then decide what should be done.

[626]   H. With regard to the length of time for which various persons are sent to different places, it would seem that, when no limitation has been set by the sovereign pontiff, the time ought to be gauged on the one hand by consideration of the nature and greater or lesser importance of the spiritual affairs in question, taking into account the need and the fruit reaped or anticipated; and on the other by consideration of what occasions emerge elsewhere, what obligation there is to respond to them, and what resources the Society possesses to provide for this or that undertaking. One should also weigh the contingencies which can intervene to shorten or lengthen the time. Finally, in view of the original design of our Institute, which is to travel through various regions, staying for longer or shorter times in accordance with the fruit that is seen, it will be necessary to judge whether it is expedient to give more time or less to certain missions or to others. So that this may be perceived, it is important that those who are sent keep the superior informed by frequent reports about the fruit which is gained.

When someone has to be moved, the superior should take care in recalling him to do everything possible to see that the persons from among whom he is taken are left quite well disposed rather than in any way disedified, and persuaded *that in everything the honor and glory of God and the universal good are being sought.*

For Prayer, Reflection, and Discussion

What reactions and reflections do I have as I ponder these texts in prayer? Have I seen such prudence in practice in the way our superiors have missioned men, including me? Is the Lord revealing anything to me (us) through my reactions and reflections on these texts?

WEEK XII, DAY 2

The Complementary Norms continue the Ignatian tradition of advocating prudent decision making and evaluation of our missions.

Preparation for Prayer: see p. 3 of this volume.

What do I desire? That God give me (us) a profound appreciation and love of our mission.

Our Mission and Criteria for Choosing Ministry, *continued*
Complementary Norms, Part VII

259   Keeping ourselves available to the Holy See above all, let all our members and especially superiors propose to themselves to follow the plans, judgments, and works of the local hierarchy; to implement them; and to be animated by the spirit and impulse toward fellowship, by which our works are harmonized with the pastoral programs of particular churches, according to the constant tradition in the Society of serving the Church by explaining, propagating, and defending the faith.

260   §1. To promote the better choice of ministries and to foresee to some extent future developments, a commission should be set up as an aid to the provincial and under his authority; the task of this commission will be, after careful study and in view of the priorities established by the general or the Conference of Major Superiors, to give advice on an overall

review of ministries. This will involve suggesting which ones ought to be kept or dropped and which others ought to be undertaken for the first time. Each year the provincial should report to Father General what has been done in this regard.

§2. In order to achieve a more effective coordination of the apostolate in a given region, the Conferences of Major Superiors can be greatly helped by a commission of the entire conference, linked with the provincial and regional commissions. In regions that are sufficiently homogeneous, a single general commission can be instituted in place of commissions for the individual provinces or regions.

261 §1. Not only should our structured activities undergo review but so should our individual apostolates, and by means of the same criteria.

§2. So that our energies may not be dispersed but instead be well organized into a single whole, superiors should bear in mind that they are placed in charge not only of their subjects themselves but also of their works. Hence, they should not be afraid to require subjects to obey them in the choice of ministries. Subjects, however, if some ministry is offered to them, should on their own initiative refer the matter to the superior, so that all is arranged in accord with his counsel. They should be willing to join their work to that of others and to subordinate themselves to others, in order to attain the more universal good.

262 The Society recognizes how apostolically important it can be for the fulfillment of our mission today that some of our members are present and work with others in certain sectors of secular activity; therefore, engaging in a secular job or profession, especially in an area that is de-Christianized or underprivileged, can at times, because of its apostolic meaning, be part of the Society's mission, provided that the mission is both given by superiors and can be carried out according to our way of proceeding.

For Prayer, Reflection, and Discussion

What reactions and reflections do I have as I ponder these texts in prayer? Do I have any questions about how my own community and/or province carry out the prescriptions of the Norms?

The first text contains the third of the three ways, according to the Constitu-
tions [603], in which a ministry is chosen. In this case the ministry is chosen
by the individual. Ignatius expects that Jesuits sent on mission will be creative
and attentive to circumstances. But for Ignatius the safer way for the Jesuit to
be sure of his mission is through contact with his superior. This section is
followed by a chapter on the ways that Jesuit communities may help their
neighbor. Note the typically Ignatian progression of these ways, from the
interior to the exterior, from the spiritual to the temporal.

Preparation for Prayer: see p. 3 of this volume.

What do I desire? That God give me (us) a profound appreciation and love of
our mission.

Our Mission and Criteria for Choosing Ministry, *continued*
A Member's Free Movement from One Place to Another
Constitutions, Part VII

[633]   1. Although it is the part of those who live under the Society's obedience not to involve themselves, directly or indirectly, with how they are sent on
mission, either by His Holiness or by their own superior in the name of Christ
our Lord, nevertheless, someone who is sent to a large territory such as the
Indies or other provinces, and for whom no particular region is assigned, may
remain for longer or shorter periods in one place or another, going off to
whatever places he deems—after having weighed the various factors, found
himself indifferent as to his will, and made his prayer—to be more expedient
for the glory of God our Lord.

From this it is clear that, without swerving from the chief and primary
obedience due to His Holiness, in missions of this type the superior will be all
the more able to direct a member to one place rather than another as he
judges in the Lord to be expedient.

[634]   2. Wherever anyone is, if he is not limited to the use of some means
such as lecturing or preaching, he may use the means which he judges more
suitable among those which the Society employs. They have been mentioned in
Part IV, chapter 8 [402–14] and will be mentioned again in the following
chapter *[A]*. Similarly, he will avoid what those passages disapprove, for the
greater service of God.

[635]   *A. However, it will always be safer for him to confer with his nearest*
superior about the means which he ought to use.

CHAPTER 4

WAYS IN WHICH THE HOUSES AND COLLEGES CAN HELP THEIR NEIGHBORS

[636]   1. Since the Society endeavors to aid its neighbors not only by traveling through various parts of the world but also by residing continually in certain places, as is the case with the houses and colleges, it is important to have a clear idea of the ways in which souls can be helped in those places, so as to put into practice those of them which are possible for the glory of God our Lord.

[637]   2. The first is by giving the good example of a thoroughly upright life and of Christian virtue, striving to edify those with whom one deals no less, but rather even more, by good deeds than by words.

[638]   3. Likewise, the neighbor is aided by desires in the presence of God our Lord and by prayers for all the Church, especially for those persons in it who are of greater importance for the common good. They should also pray for friends and benefactors, living and dead, whether they request these prayers or not; and likewise for those for whose particular benefit they and the other members of the Society are working in diverse places among believers or unbelievers, that God may dispose them all to receive his grace through the weak instruments of this least Society.

[640]   4. Furthermore, aid can be given by saying Masses and other divine services.

[642]   5. Further still, the neighbor can be aided through the administration of the sacraments, especially the hearing of confessions (with some priests being assigned by the superior for this function) and the administration of Holy Communion . . . in their church.

[645]   6. In the church the word of God should be constantly proposed to the people by means of sermons, lectures, and the teaching of Christian doctrine, by those whom the superior approves and designates for this work and at the times and in the manner which he judges to be most conducive to the greater divine glory and edification of souls.

[647]   7. The same may also be done outside the Society's church, in other churches, squares, or places of the region, when the one in charge judges it expedient for God's greater glory.

[648]   8. They will likewise endeavor to benefit individual persons in spiritual conversations, giving counsel and exhorting to good works, and in giving the Spiritual Exercises *[F]*.

[649]   *F. The Spiritual Exercises should not be given in their entirety except to a few persons, namely, those of such a character that from their progress notable fruit is expected for the glory of God. But the exercises of the First Week can be made available to large numbers; and some examinations of conscience and*

methods of prayer (especially the first of those which are touched on in the Exercises) can also be given far more widely; for anyone who has goodwill seems to be capable of these exercises.

[650]   9. They will also occupy themselves in corporal works of mercy, to the extent that the more important spiritual activities permit and their own energies allow; for example, by assistance to the sick, especially in hospitals, through visits and sending persons to serve them; by the reconciliation of quarreling parties; and likewise by doing what they can for the poor and for prisoners in the jails, both personally and by getting others to do so. How much of all this it is expedient to do will be regulated by the discretion of the superior, who will keep always in view the greater service of God and the universal good.

For Prayer, Reflection, and Discussion

What reactions and reflections do I have as I ponder these texts in prayer? Do I find my own community's actions confirmed? Do these texts raise questions about the practices of my community? Is the Lord revealing anything to me (us) by my reactions and reflections?

WEEK XII, DAY 4

The Complementary Norms selects from our recent congregations those documents that speak of the various ways in which we fulfill our mission today. Here we have the first three such ways—missionary service, interreligious dialogue, and ecumenical activity.

Preparation for Prayer: see p. 3 of this volume.

What do I desire? That God give me (us) a profound appreciation and love of our mission.

Our Mission and Criteria for Choosing Ministry, *continued*
The Ministries by Which the Society Fulfills Its Mission
Complementary Norms, Part VII

1. MISSIONARY SERVICE

263   §1. By reason of their vocation to the Society, all our members, and not only those who so petition, may be sent to evangelize peoples. But those who were born in former mission lands ought to be aware of their serious responsibility to promote the faith and the life of the Church with deep roots in their own cultures. But even they should be prepared to undertake mission service among other peoples.

§2. Superiors ought to select for the missions those who are men of solid virtue, who are quite flexible, and who are capable of fitting into a new culture, so that their proclamation of the Gospel may be sensitive to the religious situation of those to whom they address it.

264   §1. Provinces entrusted with the evangelization of peoples should consider this ministry an integral part of the province, on the same level as their other works. They should help this work with men and money, according to their means, and with a greater enthusiasm where the needs are more pressing. This applies as well to those areas that have already been erected as independent entities.

§2. Our men should diligently promote the work of evangelization of peoples among all the faithful and foster vocations for it.

2. INTERRELIGIOUS DIALOGUE

265   §1. In the context of the divisive, exploitative, and conflictual roles that religions, including Christianity, have played in history, dialogue seeks to develop the unifying and liberating potential of all religions, thus showing the relevance of religion for human well-being, justice, and world peace.

§2. Dialogue is "an activity with its own guiding principles, requirements, and dignity"; and it should never be made a strategy to elicit conversions, since a positive relationship with believers of other faiths is a requirement in a world of religious pluralism.

266   §1. The culture of dialogue should become a distinctive characteristic of our Society, sent into the whole world to labor for the greater glory of God and the help of human persons.

§2. The Society should foster the fourfold interreligious dialogue recommended by the Church; namely, "*a.* The dialogue of life, where people strive to live in an open and neighborly spirit, sharing their joys and sorrows, their human problems and preoccupations

"*b.* The dialogue of action, in which Christians and others collaborate for the integral development and liberation of people

"*c.* The dialogue of theological exchange, where specialists seek to deepen their understanding of their respective spiritual heritages and to appreciate each other's religious values

"*d.* The dialogue of religious experience, where persons who are rooted in their own religious traditions share their spiritual riches; for instance, with regard to prayer and contemplation, faith, and ways of searching for God and the Absolute"

267   The Society must prepare members able to become experts in the third aspect of interreligious dialogue. Since this dialogue is becoming a global concern, such preparation should include an interprovincial and international exchange of persons and be done in collaboration with other groups.

3. ECUMENICAL ACTIVITY

268   Faith which does justice is necessarily committed to ecumenical dialogue and cooperation. Ecumenism is not only a specific work for which some Jesuits must be trained and missioned, it is a new way of living as a Christian. It seeks, namely, what unites rather than what divides; it seeks understanding rather than confrontation, it seeks to know, understand, and love others as they wish to be known and understood, with full respect for their distinctiveness, through the dialogue of truth, justice, and love.

269   §1. In choosing the path of ecumenism, the Society is responding not only to its discernment of the signs of the times but also to the repeated calls of the Church and preceding general congregations.

§2. To foster such work, superiors should see to it that some of our members are prepared as experts in ecumenical matters according to the requirements of different regions. They are to learn to grasp fully the doctrine and the spiritual life of both Catholics and other Christians.

§3. In ecumenical activity Jesuits are faithfully to observe all the prescriptions and directives of the Holy See and of those whose duty it is to direct the ecumenical movement.

WEEK XII, DAY 5

This section takes up the fourth way of fulfilling our mission. Ignatius did not want the Society to take on the care of parishes, feeling that they would unduly hamper mobility. However, as the Complementary Norms indicate, the changing circumstances of the Church have led the Society to see a commitment to some parishes as a valuable way for the Jesuits to fulfill the mission of the Society.

Preparation for Prayer: see p. 3 of this volume.

What do I desire? That God give me (us) a profound appreciation and love of our mission.

Our Mission and Criteria for Choosing Ministry, *continued*
The Ministries by Which the Society Fulfills Its Mission, *continued*
Complementary Norms, Part VII
4. PASTORAL SERVICES AND WORKS

270   §1. Those pastoral works or services that have been initiated in the past are to be renewed and energetically promoted, provided they still fulfill the end for which they were intended and are approved by the hierarchy.

§2. According to the tradition and spirit of the Society, our members should also diligently look for new forms of pastoral services and works that answer contemporary needs, even those of other religions.

§3. Our pastoral service ought to prepare Christian communities for carrying on dialogue with believers of other religions and help them experience God's compassionate love in their lives.

271   §1. The Spiritual Exercises, carefully adapted in different ways, should be presented to every type of person insofar as individuals are capable of them, not excluding simple folk, in order to form Christians who are enriched by a personal experience of God as Savior and are led to an intimate knowledge of the Lord, so as to love and follow him more. Thus wherever necessary they can play a constructive part in the reform of social and cultural structures.

§2. The same thing should be done, as far as possible and with appropriate adaptations, for believers of other religions.

§3. Our members are to be trained to give the Spiritual Exercises in a true and correct way; others too among the diocesan and religious clergy, as well as lay women and men, are to be helped to do the same.

272   Superiors should insist that

1° The directors of works sincerely adapt themselves to contemporary pastoral practice;

2° Our members have a high esteem for teaching Christian doctrine to children and the uneducated, in accordance with the tradition of the Society and the vows they have taken; for the promotion of new forms of modern catechetics and introduction to the faith by suitable means; for the giving of spiritual assistance in hospitals and prisons;

3° Our members cooperate with the program of renewal of both the Christian Life Communities and the Apostleship of Prayer.

273   In accordance with the spirit of the Society, and especially in accordance with the repeated wish of the Church, residences should be encouraged among the more neglected groups of people. There our members should carry on their apostolate in different ways, with the special motivation that they are living their lives with the poor Christ.

274   §1. Now that the discipline of the Church in regard to parishes entrusted to religious institutes has been changed, the care of souls in a parish is no longer considered contrary to the principles of our Constitutions. In fact, under certain circumstances it can assist our mission of serving the faith and promoting justice as well as foster interreligious and cultural dialogue. It belongs to the general to judge whether any particular parishes are to be accepted or given back.

§2. Parishes accepted by the Society must be in accordance with its proper charism and mission; therefore, committed to the pastoral goals and policies of the local church, they also participate in the apostolic priorities of the Society and in the mission plan of the province, according to our way of proceeding.

§3. Those who are appointed pastors must have special training, especially in such skills as homiletics, catechesis, sociocultural analysis, social communication, and conflict management. In addition, opportunities for contact with model parishes and appropriate pastoral-training centers must be available to them for ongoing formation.

275 Worthy of particular esteem are apostolic labors among Eastern churches, whether Catholic or not Catholic, undertaken by our members by the will of the Holy See. Our members destined for this work should either retain or assume an Eastern rite, and houses and stations of an Eastern rite should be established in the Society.

276 §1. All should have a high regard for, and be keenly mindful of, the mystery of the Heart of Christ in the life of the Church. It should be so much a part of their own lives that they can promote it among others in their every apostolic activity, as a most pleasant responsibility entrusted to the Society by Christ our Lord. In this way the results of our varied ministries may daily increase.

§2. They should also trust in the patronage of the Blessed Virgin Mary in their assigned tasks and activities, and everywhere show more and more clearly the role of the mother of our Savior in the economy of salvation.

For Prayer, Reflection, and Discussion

What are my reactions as I ponder these texts in prayer? Do these texts challenge me or us to a different way of relating to parish work? If I am in parish work, do these norms relate to my experience? Is the Lord revealing anything to me (us) through my reactions and reflections?

WEEK XII, DAY 6

Preparation for Prayer: see p. 3 of this volume.

What do I desire? That God give me (us) a profound appreciation and love of our mission.

Recapitulation
Our Mission and Criteria for Choosing Ministry, *continued*

There has been a lot of material to read and ponder this week. Perhaps I can take time today to reflect on the week and on my reactions or to take up some texts that I did not have time to reflect on earlier.

WEEK XIII, DAY 1

Here the Complementary Norms take up the ministry of education in all its forms. We recall that Ignatius and the first companions did not envisage themselves as schoolmasters, but as roving apostles. Circumstances and the needs of souls determined Ignatius to send Jesuits to found the first college of the Society at Messina. Education has become one of the most important ministries of the Society. These norms take pains not to exclude any form of education nor to give preference to any form of education as a mission of the Society. Some have thought that there is an elitism among us that gives precedence to higher education. We have an opportunity to examine our own attitudes toward the various types of educational ministry.

Preparation for Prayer: see p. 3 of this volume.

What do I desire? That God give me (us) a profound appreciation and love of our mission.

Our Mission and Criteria for Choosing Ministry, *continued*
The Ministries by Which the Society Fulfills its Mission, *continued*
Complementary Norms, Part VII

5. EDUCATIONAL APOSTOLATE

a. General Remarks about the Educational Apostolate

277 §1. The educational apostolate in all its ramifications, recommended in a special way by the Church in our day, is to be valued as of great importance among the ministries of the Society for promoting today's mission in the service of faith from which justice arises. For this work, when carried out in the light of our mission, contributes greatly to

"the total and integral liberation of the human person, leading to participation in the life of God himself."

§2. Our members can exercise this apostolate in various ways either in our own institutions or by collaborating with other institutions. The Society should have its own educational institutions where resources and circumstances permit this and where there is well-grounded hope for the greater service of God and the Church.

278 Keeping intact our preferential option for the poor, we must not neglect students expected to make greater progress and to exercise greater influence on society in the service of the neighbor, no matter to what social class they belong.

279 §1. We must in a special way help prepare all our students effectively to devote themselves to building a more just world and to understand how to labor with and for others.

§2. When dealing with Christian students, we should take particular care that along with letters and sciences they acquire that knowledge and character which are worthy of Christians, and that animated by a mature faith and personally devoted to Jesus Christ, learn to find and serve him in others. For this, it will help to establish groups of Christian Life Communities in our schools.

§3. Regarding all other students of other religions, we must take care throughout the whole course of studies, and especially in the teaching of ethics courses, to form men and women who are endowed with a sound moral judgment and solid virtues.

§4. In our educational work we must sensitize our students to the value of interreligious collaboration and instill in them a basic understanding of and respect for the faith vision of those belonging to diverse local religious communities.

280 In this new communications-media culture, it is of great importance to educate our students to a critical understanding of the news transmitted by the media, so that they can learn to be selective in personally assimilating such news. Therefore, our educators should be among the best-trained people in media.

282 For its part, the Society should help those many children of the Church who are being educated in non-Catholic schools, collaborating, insofar as we are able, in directing Catholic centers for students, serving as chaplains, and also teaching in these schools.

283 We should continue to relate to and advise our former students, so that imbued with gospel values they may take their place in society and help one another in their respective tasks to work for its good.

284 To foster a close collaboration with the laity in the work of education, we should hand over to them, as far as is possible, the roles they

are prepared to assume, whether these are in teaching, in academic and financial administration, or even on the board of directors.

b. Educational institutions of the Society

285 §1. Documents on our educational apostolate, elaborated by the Central Secretariat for Education and approved by Father General, allowing for different local and cultural differences and adapted to the nature of different institutions, should inspire school mission statements, policies, teaching programs, and the entire academic milieu of the educational institutions of the Society.

§2. In order to ensure the proper character of our schools and a fruitful Jesuit-lay cooperation, it is altogether necessary to carefully select administrators and teachers, both Jesuits and others, and to form them adequately in Ignatian spirituality and pedagogy, especially those who will assume positions of major responsibility.

286 In many places, primary schools can be one of the most effective services we offer to people, especially the poor, because they can provide a solid academic and religious foundation during the formative early years.

287 §1. So-called nonformal education, by which both youths and adults are educated outside the traditional school system in both rural and urban areas of developing countries, is a very apt means to promote justice; hence, it is fully in accord with the mission of the Society and has greatly enriched it.

§2. Cooperation is to be fostered between centers for nonformal education conducted by Ours and schools, universities, and social centers of the Society, since such cooperation is beneficial to all.

288 §1. Secondary schools should improve continually both as educational institutions and as centers of culture and faith for lay collaborators, for families of students and former students, and through them for the whole community of a region. Our members should also foster close cooperation with parents of students, who bear the primary responsibility for education.

§2. Where need or great utility suggests it, other schools, such as technical and agricultural schools, may well be opened.

§3. In establishing coeducation in our secondary schools for the greater good of souls, ecclesiastical and civil norms existing in various places are to be observed.

289 §1. Universities and institutions of higher learning play an increasingly important role in the formation of the whole human community, for in them our culture is shaped by debates about ethics, future directions

for economics and politics, and the very meaning of human existence. Accordingly, we must see to it that the Society is present in such institutions, whether directed by itself or by others, insofar as we are able to do so. It is crucial for the Church, therefore, that dedicated Jesuits continue to engage in university work.

§2. We must continue to work strenuously, with imagination and faith and often under very difficult circumstances, to maintain and even to strengthen the specific character of each of our institutions of higher education both as Jesuit and as university, and bring it about that both of these aspects always remain fully operative.

§3. Universities of the Society, participating in its mission, must discover in their own proper institutional forms and authentic purposes a specific and appropriate arena, consonant with their nature, for fostering the faith that does justice.

§4. The complexity of a Jesuit university today can require new structures of government and control in order to preserve its identity and at the same time allow it to relate effectively to the academic world and the society of which it is a part, including the Society of Jesus and the Church. Periodic evaluation and accountability are necessary to judge whether or not its dynamics are being developed in line with the mission of the Society. Jesuits who work in these universities should actively involve themselves in directing them toward the objectives desired for them by the Society.

§5. A Jesuit university must be outstanding in its human, social, spiritual, and moral formation, as well as in its pastoral attention to its students and to the different groups of people who work in it or are related to it.

§6. Among the faculties of our institutions of higher learning, theology and philosophy should especially exercise their proper role, to the extent that they contribute to the greater service of God according to local circumstances. Interdisciplinary work should also be promoted, which implies a spirit of cooperation and dialogue among specialists within the university itself and with those of other universities.

290   The education of priests, as a work of the highest value, is to be considered one of the chief ministries of the Society. Therefore, seminarians who attend our universities are to be cared for with special attention, and directors and teachers chosen from among our best men are to be assigned to those clerical seminaries whose direction the Society has accepted. But if there is question of accepting diocesan seminaries, a definite agreement should be made with the bishop with the approval of Father General.'

291   Not only youth but adults also are to be educated both in advancements made in their professions and in steps that can be taken to make their conjugal, family, and social life more human and, where appropriate, more Christian and therefore just; they are to be educated also in what will serve to develop a better understanding of their own religious life.

292   Our colleges and universities may have protectors, that is, friends who undertake to protect the work; however, names connoting jurisdiction should be avoided when and where these have no place.

For Prayer, Reflection, and Discussion

What are my reactions and reflections as I ponder these texts in prayer? Do they speak to my own experience? Challenge my practice? Does the institution in which I work carry out its mission in conformity with these norms? Is the Lord revealing anything to me (us) through my reactions and reflections?

WEEK XIII, DAY 2

These texts conclude the "ways of fulfilling our mission" set down by the Complementary Norms. Taken together, these nine "ways" give us a good overview of how the recent general congregations and our recent generals are directing the Society's apostolic efforts.

Preparation for Prayer: see p. 3 of this volume.

What do I desire? That God give me (us) a profound appreciation and love of our mission.

6. INTELLECTUAL APOSTOLATE

293   §1. Research in philosophy and theology, in the other sciences and in every branch of human culture is extremely necessary to fulfill our mission today and to help the Church to understand the contemporary world and speak to it the Word of salvation.

§2. Ours whom superiors assign to this scholarly work are to give themselves to it entirely and with a strong and self-denying spirit, for in one way or another such work makes demands upon the whole person. They should know that they are making an invaluable contribution to the contemporary mission of the Society. At the same time they should do this in such a way that they do not lose touch with other apostolic activities of the Society and should cooperate with our members who are engaged in more direct social and pastoral ministries.

294   Among all the ways of being engaged in the intellectual apostolate in the service of the Kingdom of God, theological research and reflection, when undertaken with the seriousness of research and the creativity of imagination that they merit, within the broad spectrum of Catholic theology and in the midst of the varied circumstances in which Jesuits live and work, have a special place because of their unique value to discern, illuminate, and interpret the opportunities and problems of contemporary life and thus to respond to the broadest questions of the human mind and the deepest yearnings of the human heart.

295   In the elaboration and expression of our theological views and in our choice of pastoral options, we must always actively seek to understand the mind of the hierarchical Church, having as our goal the Society's objective to help souls. At the same time, we must try to articulate the *sensus fidelium* and help the magisterium discern in it the movements of the Spirit in accord with the teaching of Vatican II.

296   The office of writer should be regarded as a ministry that is most profitable to souls and altogether appropriate to the Society; therefore, it is to be diligently encouraged by superiors. Regulations enacted both by the common law of the Church and our own Institute with regard to the publishing of books should be exactly and fairly put into practice.

297   We must never forget the distinctive importance of the intellectual quality of all our ministries. Therefore we must all insist on the ongoing development of our capacity to analyze and evaluate our mission, which is indispensable if we wish to integrate the promotion of justice with the

proclamation of faith, and if we hope to be effective in our work for peace, in our concern to protect life and the environment, in our defense of the rights of individual men and women and of entire peoples.

7. SOCIAL APOSTOLATE

298   In the planning of our apostolic activities, in fulfilling today's mission of the Society in the service of faith, the social apostolate should take its place among those of prime importance. Its goal is to build, by means of every endeavor, a fuller expression of justice and charity into the structures of human life in common.

299   §1. The social apostolate, like every form of our apostolate, flows from the mission "for the defense and propagation of the faith and the progress of souls in Christian life and learning."

§2. Moreover, all should understand that they can and ought to exercise the social apostolate in their spiritual ministries by explaining the social teaching of the Church, by stimulating and directing the souls of the faithful toward social justice and social charity, and, finally, by establishing social projects by means of the members of our organizations.

300   §1. Provinces or regions should sponsor social centers for research, publications, and social action according to a plan that will seem better suited to the concrete circumstances of each region and time. They should be in close contact with one another both to garner information and to supply every kind of practical collaboration; and in particular to identify and promote the liberating dynamics of the local religions and cultures, and to initiate common projects for the building of a just social order.

§2. Social centers and direct social action for and with the poor will be more effective in promoting justice to the extent that they integrate faith into all dimensions of their work.

301   §1. Our members should promote those things that, in the light of the social teaching of the Church, tend to infuse Christian principles into public life; they should not, however, become involved in partisan politics.

§2. Whether any of our members, in truly exceptional circumstances, may be permitted to take some active part in offices entailing a participation in the exercise of civil power or in political parties or in the direction of labor unions is for the general to decide; he will take into account the universal law of the Church and the opinion of competent ecclesiastical authority.

302   In the entire course of our training, both theoretical (by serious study of the social sciences) and practical, the social dimension of our whole modern apostolate must be taken into account and members who

are to be specifically destined for this apostolate should be chosen in good time and appropriately trained.

8. SOCIAL COMMUNICATIONS

303 §1. The Society should acknowledge that communication is not primarily a sector restricted to a few Jesuit "professionals," but rather a major apostolic dimension of all our apostolates. Therefore, every Jesuit, in order to be apostolically effective, must be aware of and well versed in the language and symbols, as well as the strengths and weaknesses, of modern communication culture.

§2. We must cooperate with the media, so that the Church's true face can appear and the Gospel can be inculturated in this new mass culture as well. Though we remain always loyal to the truth, our Ignatian sense of *sentire cum ecclesia* will lead us to present what is praiseworthy in the Church.

§3. In no way detracting from the general formation to be given to all, according to no. 96, §2, in order that we may more efficaciously use the social-communications media in a way that is adapted to the needs and opportunities of our apostolate in fulfilling our mission, major superiors should in good time choose and assign some men endowed with a religious spirit and other gifts, so that after they have become expert at various levels of specialization and have acquired academic degrees, they may become competent in practicing these skills and in directing others.

9. INTERPROVINCIAL WORKS AND HOUSES IN ROME

304 §1. In the spirit of our fourth vow, the Society confirms its commitment to the interprovincial Roman works entrusted to it by the Holy See: the Pontifical Gregorian University and its associated institutes, the Pontifical Biblical Institute and the Pontifical Oriental Institute; as well as the Pontifical Russicum College, the Vatican Radio, and the Vatican Observatory, all of which are common works of the whole Society, placed directly under the superior general. Recognizing the very valuable service that these institutions have offered and continue to offer today, it calls upon major superiors who share Father General's responsibility for them to continue their help through subsidies and especially by training and offering professors and other personnel to them.

§2. Also recommended to the care of all the provinces are those other works or houses in Rome that render a service to the entire Society, such as the Historical Institute of the Society of Jesus and the international colleges of the Society in Rome.

WEEK XIII, DAY 3

It has been noted that the Church is experiencing the coming of age of the laity as full-fledged actors in its life and ministry. The Complementary Norms ask us to reflect on our attitudes and our practice with regard to cooperation with the laity.

Preparation for Prayer: see p. 3 of this volume.

What do I desire? That God give me (us) a profound appreciation and love of our mission.

Our Mission and Criteria for Choosing Ministry, *continued*
Our Cooperation with the Laity in Mission
Complementary Norms, Part VII, Chapter 5

1. Cooperation with the Laity in General

305   §1. The Society recognizes as a grace of our day and a hope for the future the laity's taking "an active, conscientious, and responsible part in the mission of the Church in this great moment of history." Therefore, we seek to respond to this grace by cooperating with them to realize their mission fully, accommodating ourselves in our way of conceiving and exercising "our" apostolate.

§2. In order to achieve this, all our members should become more keenly aware of the meaning of the state and vocation of the laity and their apostolate in the Church and the world, according to the new teaching of the ecclesiastical magisterium. By means of fraternal dialogue with them, we should make efforts to understand better their life, their ways of thinking and feeling, their aspirations and their religious mentality; and along with them we should strive to share our spiritual heritage, conscious that we can receive from the laity much to strengthen our own vocation and mission.

2. Cooperation with the Laity in Their Works

306 §1. The Society places itself at the service of the mission of the laity by offering them what we are and have received; namely, formation in our apostolic spirituality, especially—to the extent this is desired—the experience of the Spiritual Exercises and spiritual direction and discernment, educational resources for developing their pastoral and apostolic capacities, and our friendship.

§2. We intend to cooperate with them as true companions, serving together, learning from and responding to each other's concerns and initiatives, dialoguing with one another on apostolic objectives, always ready to serve as counselors, assistants, or helpers in works that the laity promote.

§3. For our part, this cooperation in these works should be in accord with the Society's criteria for the choice of ministries, especially service of the faith and promotion of justice and the other integral dimensions of our mission; our members should be missioned to this cooperative work with clear apostolic objectives and should remain in continuous discernment with their superior and apostolic community.

§4. This cooperation requires from all of us formation and renewal, to take place early in our training and throughout our lives. By means of this we will be aided both in understanding and respecting the distinctive lay vocation as well as in appreciating our own.

For Prayer, Reflection, and Discussion

What are my reactions and reflections as I ponder these texts in prayer? This may be an appropriate time for an examen of consciousness before God of my attitudes toward cooperation with the laity. I may discover in myself resistance to sharing ministry with laity; if I do, then I have something to talk over with the Lord. I can ask him to help me to take on his mind and heart. Am I (are we) willing to be servants of the mission of lay people? Is the Lord revealing something to me (us) through my reactions and reflections?

WEEK XIII, DAY 4

In this passage we reflect on our working relations with laity in institutions sponsored by the Society.

Preparation for Prayer: see p. 3 of this volume.

What do I desire? That God give me (us) a profound appreciation and love of our mission.

Our Mission and Criteria for Choosing Ministry, *continued*
Our Cooperation with the Laity in Mission, *continued*
Complementary Norms, Part VII, Chapter 5

3. Cooperation with the Laity in Works of the Society

307   §1. Cooperation with the laity in works of the Society, namely, those works whereby the Society realizes its mission, manifests Ignatian values, and in various ways assumes and retains "ultimate responsibility," must be guided by a clear mission statement that outlines the purposes of the work and forms the basis for collaboration in it. This mission statement should be proposed and clearly explained to all those with whom we cooperate.

§2. Programs are to be provided to enable these lay people to acquire a greater knowledge of the Ignatian tradition and spirituality and to grow in their personal vocations.

§3. We must not only fully observe the demands of justice toward those who work with us but also maintain a cordial cooperation based on love. We must open up to them in various ways a wide participation in, as well as responsibility for, the organization, implementation, and administration of our works, presupposing that our coworkers have assimilated the principles of Ignatian spirituality which inspire our mission; of course, we must also keep the power of ultimate decision in the hands of the Society where it has the ultimate responsibility.

§4. Where these conditions are verified, a lay person can be the director of a work of the Society. When this is the case, members of the Society receive from the provincial their mission to work in the institution, and they carry out this mission under the direction of the lay director. In institutions where Jesuits are a small minority, special attention should be given both to the leadership role of lay colleagues and to appropriate means for the Society to assure the Jesuit identity of the work.

308   In order to foster the responsibility of the laity in the Church, the Society should examine at the proper moment whether some works

begun by us might be turned over to competent lay men and women for the greater good of the Church.

For Prayer, Reflection, and Discussion

What are my reactions and reflections as I ponder these texts in prayer? This may be an appropriate time for an examen of consciousness before God of my attitudes toward cooperation with the laity. I may discover in myself resistance to sharing ministry with laity; if I do, then I have something to talk over with the Lord. I can ask him to help me to take on his mind and heart. Are there works that we should be planning to hand over to lay people? Is the Lord revealing something to me (us) through my reactions and reflections?

WEEK XIII, DAY 5

Preparation for Prayer: see p. 3 of this volume.

What do I desire? That God give me (us) a profound appreciation and love of our mission.

Our Mission and Criteria for Choosing Ministry, *continued*
Our Cooperation with the Laity in Mission, *continued*
Complementary Norms, Part VII, Chapter 5

4. Lay Associations of Ignatian Inspiration

309   §1. Many lay persons desire to be united with us through participation in apostolic associations of Ignatian inspiration. The Society views positively this growth of lay associations. They give witness to the Ignatian charism in the world, enable us to undertake with them works of greater dimensions, and help their members to live the faith more fully. The Society encourages its members to study these various associations, to know them through personal contact, and to develop a genuine interest in them.

§2. Among such associations the Society actively promotes and fosters with special care the following, and it encourages provinces to do the same: Christian Life Communities, Jesuit Volunteers and similar programs, Jesuit Former Student Associations, the Apostleship of Prayer, and the Eucharistic Youth Movement, recommended by the Holy See. This list does not in any way intend to exclude other communities or movements with which the Society has very privileged and fruitful links in a number of countries.

§3. That so many persons share with us the inspiration of Ignatian spirituality as they realize their own lay vocation in the Church impels us to work with them more decisively, so that after careful discernment we may strengthen the organic bonds among all these persons and groups. Thus we will foster better communication and provide stronger personal and spiritual support among them and provide an example of the sort of specific contribution the Society can make to "the new evangelization."

5. Closer Bonds of Certain Laity with the Society

310   One possibility among others for the Society to cooperate with the laity in mission is to set up a special personal "juridical bonding" of certain persons, whether or not they form an association among themselves, for the attainment of apostolic purposes. Such experimentation is recommended, according to directions given by the general congregation, and should be evaluated in the future.

For Prayer, Reflection, and Discussion

What are my reactions and reflections as I ponder these texts in prayer? What is my experience with groups such as the Christian Life Community or the Jesuit Volunteer Corps? If I have little contact with such groups, am I called to have more? Am I called to find out what my province is doing with such groups? Do I sense any positive or negative movements regarding the possibility of my province experimenting with a special personal "juridical bonding" with specific lay persons such as the Wisconsin Province has done? What is the Lord revealing to me (us) through my reactions and reflections?

WEEK XIII, DAY 6

Preparation for Prayer: see p. 3 of this volume.

What do I desire? That God give me (us) a profound appreciation and love of our mission.

Our Mission and Criteria for Choosing Ministry, *continued*
Recapitulation

For Prayer, Reflection, and Discussion

As I look back over the prayer of the past week, what stands out? What do I want to talk over with my group? Is the Lord calling us to anything different either in our way of acting or in our ministry itself?

WEEK XIV, DAY 1

Part VIII of the Constitutions and of the Complementary Norms treats of the means of fostering the union of minds and hearts in the Society. Ignatius was very practical about the dangers of disunity. Note the sources of disunity that he writes of, especially the hint of the possibility of jealousy in no. 656. Ignatius knew well that Jesuits are sinners called to be companions of Christ. Ignatius also saw the union of minds and hearts in the Society as having apostolic value. We are companions of Jesus for mission.

Preparation for Prayer: see p. 3 of this volume.

What do I desire? That God give me (us) a profound appreciation and love of our Society and of its members.

Helps Toward Uniting the Dispersed Members with Their Head and among Themselves

Aids toward the Union of Hearts

Constitutions, Part VIII, Chapter 1

[655] 1. The more difficult it is for the members of this congregation to be united with their head and among themselves, since they are so spread out in diverse parts of the world among believers and unbelievers *[A]*, the more should means be sought for that union. For the Society cannot be preserved or governed or, consequently, attain the aim it seeks for the greater glory of God unless its members are united among themselves and with their head. Therefore the present treatise will deal first with means towards the union of hearts, and then towards the union of persons in congregations or chapters. With respect to the union of hearts, some things will be helpful on the side of the subjects, others on the side of the superiors, and others on both sides.

[656] *A. There are also other reasons, for example, the fact that they will ordinarily be learned men who enjoy the favor of princes or important persons, or of peoples, and so forth.*

Union of Minds and Hearts

Complementary Norms, Part VIII, Chapter 1

311 §1. Our members fulfill their mission in companionship with others, for they belong to a community of friends in the Lord who have desired to be received under the standard of Christ the King.

§2. It is our community-life ideal that we should be not only fellow workers in the apostolate but truly brothers and friends in Christ.

312 Given the wide dispersion of our apostolic enterprises, the need for us to acquire highly specialized skills for highly specialized works, and in many places the need to make a distinction between our apostolic institutions and our religious communities, the preservation of unity of purpose and direction becomes a prime necessity.

313 §1. Within limits imposed by our profession of poverty, communication and union among members of the Society should be strengthened in the following ways, besides those other useful ways already begun:

a. Gatherings of communities in the same city or region or in the whole province should be encouraged;

b. Task forces and workshops for reflection should be established in the provinces for each area of the apostolate or, where it can easily and usefully be done, also among provinces;

c. The superiors of each province and the provincials of each assistancy or major region should hold regular meetings.

§2. What especially helps toward fostering communion among all members of the Society is an attitude of mind and heart that esteems and welcomes each member as a brother and friend in the Lord, because "[w]hat helps most . . . toward this end must be, more than any exterior constitution, the interior law of love and charity which the Holy Spirit writes and engraves in our hearts."

For Prayer, Reflection, and Discussion

What are my reactions and reflections as I ponder these texts in prayer? Am I reminded of any antipathy in me toward other members? What have I done to try to overcome this source of disunity? The Society has undergone a tremendous upheaval since Vatican II. Are there in me and in my community or province residual scars that mar our unity? Is the Lord revealing anything to me (us) by my reactions to these texts?

WEEK XIV, DAY 2

Once again Ignatius returns to the issue of selectivity in accepting and retaining members in the Society. Here he points to the dangers to unity posed by difficult persons. Ignatius writes from experience, as we know from his dealings with Simão Rodrigues and Nicolás Bobadilla. We note again Ignatius's insistence on obedience, but here as a source of union of hearts and minds in the Society. It was because of disturbances of unity in the Portuguese Province that Ignatius wrote his famous letter on obedience in 1553.

Preparation for Prayer: see p. 3 of this volume.

What do I desire? That God give me (us) a profound appreciation and love of our Society and of its members.

Aids toward the Union of Hearts
Constitutions, Part VIII

[657]   2. On the side of the subjects, it will be helpful not to admit a mob of persons to profession, and to retain only selected persons even to be formed coadjutors or scholastics *[B]* [Approved brothers are included with the scholastics according to *CN* no. 6]. For a crowd of persons whose vices are not well mortified is incapable of order and likewise of unity, so necessary in Christ our Lord for preserving the Society's well-being and proper functioning.

[658]   *B. This is not to exclude even a large number of persons suitable for profession or admission as formed coadjutors or approved scholastics. Rather, the injunction is against too easily passing as suitable those persons who are not, especially for admission among the professed. If what was stated in Parts I and V is properly observed, it will suffice; such persons, even if numerous, would be considered a select group, not a mob.*

[659]   3. Since this union is produced in great part by the bond of obedience, this virtue should always be maintained in its vigor; and those who are sent out from the houses to labor in the Lord's field should as far as possible be persons practiced in this virtue. Those who are more important in the Society should give a good example of obedience to the others, by being closely united to their own superior and by obeying him promptly, humbly, and devoutly. Thus too one who has not given much evidence of this virtue ought at least to go in the company of someone who has, for in general a companion more advanced in obedience will help one who is less so, with the divine favor.

[662]   4. To the virtue of obedience also pertains the properly observed subordination of some superiors to others and of subjects to superiors, in such wise that the individuals who dwell in a house or college have recourse to their local superior or rector and are governed by him in all things. Those who are spread throughout the province refer to the provincial or another local superior who is closer, according to the orders they have received; and all the local superiors or rectors should communicate often with the provincial and thus too be directed by him in everything; and the provincials in their turn will deal in the same way with the general. This subordination, when thus observed, will uphold union, which to a very great extent consists therein, with the grace of God our Lord.

[664]   5. Anyone seen to be a cause of division among those who live together, estranging them either among themselves or from their head, ought with great diligence to be separated from that community, as a pestilence which can infect it seriously if a remedy is not quickly applied *[F]*.

[665]   *F. To separate can mean either expelling the person from the Society altogether or transferring him to another place if this seems sufficient and more expedient for the divine service and the common good in the judgment of the one responsible for it.*

WEEK XIV, DAY 3

These texts continue Ignatius's reflections on obedience as the Society's way to unity. What is said about the superior general also applies to provincials and local superiors. It is interesting that Ignatius's mystical vision for the Society sees the graces of the Society being communicated through union with the superior general.

Preparation for Prayer: see p. 3 of this volume.

What do I desire? That God give me (us) a profound appreciation and love of our Society and of its members.

Aids toward the Union of Hearts
Constitutions, Part VIII

[666]   6. On the side of the superior general, what will aid toward this union of hearts are the qualities of his person *[G],* to be treated in Part IX [723–25], with which he will perform his office, which is to be for all the members a head from which the influence required for the end sought by the Society ought to descend to them all. It is thus from the general as head that all authority of the provincials should flow, from the provincials that of the local superiors, and from the local superiors that of the individual members. And from this same head, or at least by his commission and approval, should likewise come the appointing of missions. And the same should apply to communicating the graces of the Society. For the more the subjects are dependent upon their superiors, the better will the love, obedience, and union among them be preserved.

[667]   G. *Very especially helpful, among other qualities, will be his credit and prestige among his subjects, as well as his having and showing love and concern for them, in such a way that the subjects hold the opinion that their superior has the knowledge, desire, and ability to rule them well in our Lord. For this and many other matters he will find it useful to have with him persons able to give good counsel (as will be stated in Part IX [803, 804]), whose help he can employ in what he needs to ordain for the Society's good proceeding in various different regions for the divine glory.*

It will further help if his commanding is well thought out and ordered; he should endeavor to keep up obedience among the subjects in such wise that the superior on his part employs all possible love, modesty, and charity in our Lord so that the subjects may be disposed always to have greater love than fear for their superiors, though at times both are useful. He should also leave some matters up to them when it appears likely they will be helped by this; and at other times he should go along with them in part and sympathize with them when this might seem best.

[671]   8. On both sides, the chief bond to cement the union of the members among themselves and with their head is the love of God our Lord. For when the superior and the subjects are closely united to his Divine and Supreme Goodness, they will very easily be united among themselves, through that same love which will descend from the Divine Goodness and spread to all other persons, and particularly to the body of the Society. Thus charity will come to further this union between superiors and subjects, and in general all goodness and virtues through which one proceeds in conformity with the spirit. Consequently there will be also total contempt of temporal things, in regard to which self-love, the chief enemy of this union and universal good, frequently induces disorder.

Still another great help can be found in uniformity, both interior uniformity of doctrine, judgments, and wills, as far as this is possible *[K]*, and exterior uniformity in respect to clothing, ceremonies of the Mass, and other such matters, to the extent that the different qualities of persons, places, and the like permit.

[672]   K. *In the case of those who have not studied, it is good to strive that all normally follow a single doctrine, that selected in the Society as the best and most suitable for its members. A person who has already finished his studies should also take care to keep diversity from harming the union of charity, and to accommodate himself in what is possible to the doctrine that is more common in the Society.*

WEEK XIV, DAY 4

The Complementary Norms emphasize that in the Society community life is for the sake of mission. At the same time they underline that it is a life in common, a life of friendship in the Lord. The first companions really loved one another; it was the needs of God's people, that is, their mission, that led them to move away from one another, not a lack of close friendship. Just as a Jesuit may have to cut short time for prayer for the sake of mission, so too he may have to tear himself away from his close friends in the Society for the sake of mission. But Ignatius assumed that a Jesuit would want to pray a great deal and that a Jesuit would love his brothers in Christ and want to be with them.

Preparation for Prayer: see p. 3 of this volume.

What do I desire? That God give me (us) a profound appreciation and love of our Society and of its members.

Community Life of the Society

Complementary Norms, Part VIII, Chapter 2

314   §1. Community in the Society of Jesus takes its origin from the will of the Father joining us into one; it is constituted by the active, personal, united striving of all members to fulfill the divine will and is ordered to a life that is apostolic in many ways.

§2. Our community is the entire body of the Society itself, no matter how widely dispersed over the face of the earth. The particular local community to which one belongs at any given moment is, for him, simply a concrete—if, here and now, a privileged—expression of this worldwide brotherhood.

315   A local Jesuit community is an apostolic community, whose focus of concern is the service that Ours are bound, in virtue of their vocation, to give to people. It is a community *ad dispersionem,* since its members are ready to go wherever they are sent; but it is also a *koinonia,* a close sharing of life and goods, with the Eucharist at its center, and a community of discernment with superiors, to whom belong the final steps in making decisions about undertaking and accomplishing missions.

316   §1. When community life flourishes, the whole religious life is sound; and unity and availability, universality, full personal dedication, and gospel freedom are also strengthened for the assistance of souls in every way.

§2. Community life itself is a manifold testimony for our contemporaries, especially since it fosters brotherly love and unity by which all will know that we are disciples of Christ.

317   The more one is exposed to situations and structures alien to the faith, the more one must strengthen his own religious identity and his union with the whole body of the Society as represented by the local community to which he belongs. Therefore, all our members, even those who must live apart because of the demands of their apostolate or for other justifiable reasons, should take an active part as far as possible in the life of some community.

318   Every community of the Society should have its own superior, who should maintain it in love and obedience.

For Prayer, Reflection, and Discussion

What are my reactions and reflections as I ponder these texts in prayer? Is my own experience confirmed by these texts? Am I challenged to any changes in my community life? What about my own community life? Is God revealing anything to me (us) through my reactions and reflections?

WEEK XIV, DAY 5

As we reflect on Ignatius's norms on communication, we need to remember the conditions of those days. All letters had to be written and copied by hand, and, to ensure delivery, often enough several copies had to be sent by various routes. Letters from Ignatius to Francis Xavier, for example, could take several years to arrive. Given the difficulties and time involved in writing and sending letters, it is amazing how insistent Ignatius was on letter writing and how many letters he wrote. It shows how much he valued personal knowledge of his brethren and communication between Jesuits to ensure union of minds and hearts.

Preparation for Prayer: see p. 3 of this volume.

What do I desire? That God give me (us) a profound appreciation and love of our Society and of its members.

Aids toward the Union of Hearts
Constitutions, Part VIII

[673]   9. Another very special help will be communication by letter between subjects and superiors *[L]*, and their learning frequently about one another and hearing the news *[M]* and reports *[N]* which come from the various regions. The superiors, especially the general and the provincials, will take charge of this, making arrangements so that each region can learn from the others whatever promotes mutual consolation and edification in our Lord.

[674]   *L. The local superiors or rectors in a province, and those who are sent to bear fruit in the Lord's field, should write to their provincial superior once a week if facilities for this exist. The provincial and the others should likewise write to the general every week if he is near. If they are in a different kingdom where such facilities are lacking, both the said persons who have been sent to bear fruit as well as the local superiors and rectors will, like the provincials, write once a month to the general. The general will have a letter written to them ordinarily once a month, at least to the provincials; and the provincials once a month to the local superiors, rectors, and individuals where this is required; and more frequently from one side and the other as need for this may arise in our Lord.*

[675]   *M. So that news about the Society can be communicated to everyone, the following procedure should be followed. At the beginning of every four-month period, those under a provincial who is over various houses or colleges should write a letter containing only matters of edification in the vernacular language of the province, as well as another of the same tenor in Latin. They should send the provincial two copies of each, so that he can send one copy of the Latin and the vernacular to the general, along with a letter of his own stating anything noteworthy or edifying that was not mentioned by the individuals, and can have the*

second recopied as often as is needed to inform the others of his own province. In cases where much time would be lost by sending these letters to the provincial, local superiors and rectors may send their Latin and vernacular letters directly to the general, with a copy to the provincial. Also, when the provincial thinks it advisable he may charge some of the local superiors with informing the others in his province by sending them copies of what they write to the provincial.

However, so that what pertains to one province may be known in another, the general will order that sufficient copies of the letters sent to him from the provinces should be made to provide for all the other provincials; and these provincials will likewise have copies made for the members of their own province.

[676]   *N. For fuller knowledge of everyone, every four months the provincial should be sent, from each house and college, a brief list in duplicate of all who are in that house, and of those who are now missing because of death or some other cause, from the time of the last list sent until the date of the present one, with a brief account of the qualities of these persons. In the same manner, every four months the provincial will send to the general the copies of the lists from each house and college. For in this way it will be possible to have more information about the persons and to govern the whole body of the Society better, for the glory of God our Lord.*

For Prayer, Reflection, and Discussion

What are my reactions and reflections as I ponder these texts in prayer? What is my own practice of communication? How have modern methods of communication affected me (us)? Do I experience the Society (Roman Curia, province curia, community, companions in my apostolate, friends) as communicators according to the mind of Ignatius? Is God revealing anything to me (us) through my reactions and reflections?

WEEK XIV, DAY 6

These texts will serve as a focus for the recapitulation of this week, which has focused on the union of minds and hearts.

Preparation for Prayer: see p. 3 of this volume.

What do I desire? That God give me (us) a profound appreciation and love of our Society and of its members.

Community Life of the Society
Complementary Norms, Part VIII

319   The following are necessary for fostering community life in the Society of Jesus: exchange of information between superiors and subjects; consultation by which experts share their insights and all members of the community actively engage in the process of coordinating and promoting the apostolate and other things that pertain to the good of the community; delegation by superiors in favor of their subjects; collaboration of various kinds transcending every sort of individualism; a certain daily order; a feeling for the whole Society on the part of its members that transcends local and personal limits.

320   All should associate with one another easily, in sincerity, evangelical simplicity, and courtesy, as is appropriate for a family gathered together in the name of the Lord.

For Prayer, Reflection, and Discussion

What are my reactions and reflections as I ponder these texts in prayer? Do these norms characterize my community, my province, my own interactions with my Jesuit brothers? What stands out as I look back over my notes for this week? Is the Lord revealing anything to me (us) through my reactions and reflections?

WEEK XV, DAY 1

The Complementary Norms spell out for our time some particulars of our common life that foster union of minds and hearts.

Preparation for Prayer: see p. 3 of this volume.

What do I desire? That God give me (us) a profound appreciation and love of our Society and of its members.

Union of Minds and Hearts, *continued*
Community Life of the Society, *continued*
Complementary Norms, Part VIII, Chapter 2

321   The standard of living with regard to food, clothing, and furniture should be common to all, so that, poor in fact and in spirit, differences may be avoided as far as possible. This does not prevent each one from having what is necessary for his work or for his health, with the permission of the superior.

322   Customs that are more suitable for monastic life are not to be introduced into our community life, nor those that are proper to seculars; much less should those that manifest a worldly spirit. Let our relationship with all other men and women be such as can rightly be expected from men consecrated to God and seeking the good of souls above all things, and such as includes a proper regard for genuine fellowship with all our members.

323   Since our communities are apostolic, they should be oriented to the service of others, particularly the poor, and to cooperation with those seeking God or working for greater justice in the world. For this reason, under the leadership of superiors, communities should periodically examine whether their way of living supports their apostolic mission sufficiently and encourages hospitality. They should also consider whether their style of life testifies to simplicity, justice, and poverty.

For Prayer, Reflection, and Discussion

What are my reactions and reflections as I ponder these texts in prayer? What about my own common life? What about our common life in community? In the province? Am I (Are we) being challenged by any of these norms? Is the Lord revealing anything to me (us) through my reactions and reflections?

Week XV, Day 2

Note here that the community is described as apostolic, involved most often in a work external to itself, yet at the same time as having an internal life to which each member is asked to contribute.

Preparation for Prayer: see p. 3 of this volume.

What do I desire? That God give me (us) a profound appreciation and love of our Society and of its members.

Union of Minds and Hearts, *continued*
Community Life of the Society, *continued*
Complementary Norms, Part VIII, Chapter 2

324 §1. To the extent possible, superiors should strive to build an Ignatian apostolic community in which many forms of open and friendly communication on a spiritual level are possible.

§2. Taking into account the mission it has been given, every community should after mature deliberation under the direction of the superior establish a daily order for community life, to be approved by the provincial and periodically reviewed.

§3. The daily order of the community should include, besides a brief prayer every day as mentioned in no. 230, occasionally a longer period for prayerful discussion; when the will of God is seriously sought concerning the life and work of the community, elements of true spiritual discernment in common can be included.

325 §1. Each member should contribute to community life and give sufficient time and effort to the task. Only in this way can a certain "atmosphere" be created that makes communication possible and in which no one is neglected or looked down upon.

§2. As far as apostolic work or other occupations for the greater glory of God permit it, all of us, "esteeming the others in their hearts as better than themselves," should be ready to help out in the common household chores.

WEEK XV, DAY 3

In these texts the Complementary Norms ask the Society to face the question of union of hearts and minds in terms of the relations between priests and brothers. The treatment of brothers in the Society has not always been brotherly. In addition, some of us remember that men who had college degrees but who felt called to be brothers found themselves pushed to consider becoming priests, the implication being that they were too well educated to be content to be brothers. We have a chance with this reflection to ponder our own attitudes toward one another and to ask the Lord's help to heal any wounds that still fester and any attitudes that run counter to our common brotherhood in Christ.

Preparation for Prayer: see p. 3 of this volume.

What do I desire? That God give me (us) a profound appreciation and love of our Society and of its members.

Union of Minds and Hearts, *continued*

Community Life of the Society, *continued*

Complementary Norms, Part VIII, Chapter 2

326   §1. As the most effective means of strengthening the sense of being part of one mission and of increasing the high regard we have for one another, fraternal union and communication are to be fostered more and more among all our members (priests, scholastics, and brothers) by all the means that a discerning love may dictate.

§2. To achieve more effectively the integration and participation of brothers in the common vocation and mission of the Society, important changes have been introduced in our proper law.

§3. Communities that include priests, brothers, and scholastics are to be encouraged. If everyone in them shares in all aspects of community life, including faith, domestic tasks, relaxation, prayer, apostolic discernment, the Eucharist, and the Spiritual Exercises, more and more we will truly become "friends in the Lord." This sharing of life will help to build up communities of shared responsibility in our common following of Jesus and complementarity in the one mission. To make this sharing a reality among us, we need human and spiritual maturity and a better formation in interpersonal communication.

§4. To this end it will also be conducive

a. To give brothers a share in consultations

b. To observe what is set down about participation of brothers in congregations and about assigning to them offices of direction

c. In the future to use the term "brother" or "Jesuit brother," but not the term "temporal coadjutor," in our official or ordinary texts.

For Prayer, Reflection, and Discussion

What are my reactions and reflections as I ponder these norms in prayer? What are my own attitudes toward the vocation of brothers in the Society? Are there any festering wounds in me? Any attitudes that show a bias against brothers? Would I encourage a man to become a brother in the Society of Jesus today? Is the Lord revealing anything to me (us) through my reactions and reflections?

WEEK XV, DAY 4

These are the final norms on community life in the Complementary Norms.

Preparation for Prayer: see p. 3 of this volume.

What do I desire? That God give me (us) a profound appreciation and love of our Society and of its members.

Union of Minds and Hearts, *continued*
Community Life of the Society, *continued*
Complementary Norms, Part VIII, Chapter 2

327   §1. Keeping in mind apostolic poverty and our witness to those among whom we must live, our houses should be made suitable for apostolic work, study, prayer, relaxation of mind, and a friendly spirit, so that our members will feel at home in their own house and so more efficaciously carry on our apostolic mission.

§2. In our houses a certain part should be reserved for our members, in which enclosure adapted to our mission is to be observed. This is to be fully observed in houses yet to be built; in houses that have already been constructed, it is to be carried out as far as possible.

§3. Ours should be mindful that a quite generous hospitality toward our own men rightly figures among the primary and most effective causes of mutual union among ourselves; therefore, our houses should never cease to be open and welcoming to Ours. Our houses should also be open in genuine hospitality to others, especially to religious and to those who work with us, according to the customs in different places.

328   No one should spend a notable period of time outside the house without the permission of at least the local superior.

329   Solidarity among all communities in a province or region, which should also extend beyond their limits, as well as fraternal charity require that communities be open to men of different ages, talent, and work.

330   Particular norms, adapted to local circumstances, that are to be observed in the houses of a province or region can be determined by individual provincials or by a regional group of provincials, with the approval of the general; if they are published, all the major superiors to whom they apply should maintain them with equal vigor.

For Prayer, Reflection, and Discussion

What are my reactions and reflections as I ponder these norms in prayer? Am I happy with my own community's hospitality toward Jesuits and others? With my own hospitality toward Jesuits and others? Is the Lord revealing anything to me (us) through my reactions and reflections?

WEEK XV, DAY 6

For this day of recapitulation I have chosen some texts about the manner of conducting business in a general congregation. Ignatius presumes that God has an interest in what happens in a general congregation. He even takes into account an election of a general superior in a way analogous to an election in the "first time" in the Spiritual Exercises [no. 175] where the inspiration of God is so palpable that there can be no doubt about the course of action to be taken. Ignatius, throughout the Constitutions, keeps in mind God and the need to try to discern God's desires for us.

Preparation for Prayer: see p. 3 of this volume.

What do I desire? That God give me (us) a profound appreciation and love of our Society and of its members.

Union of Minds and Hearts, *continued*
Manner of Electing a General Superior
Constitutions, Part VIII

[697]   3. On the day of the election, which will be that following the three mentioned, the Mass of the Holy Spirit should be said, and all should attend and receive Communion.

[698]   4. Later at the sound of the bell those with the right to vote should be summoned to the place of assembly. One of them should deliver a sermon in which he exhorts them in a general way, with no suggestion of alluding to any individual, to choose a superior such as is required for the greater divine service. After all together have recited the hymn "Veni Creator Spiritus," they should be locked inside the place of the congregation by one of the superiors or rectors or another member of the Society charged with this in the house where the assembly is held. They are enclosed in such a manner that they may not leave nor be given any food except bread and water until they have elected a general.

[700]   5. If all by a common inspiration should choose someone without waiting for the voting procedure, let him be the superior general, for the Holy Spirit who has moved them to such an election supplies for all procedures and arrangements.

[701]   6. When the election does not take place in that manner, the following procedure should be followed. First, each one should pray privately and, without speaking with anyone else, make his decision in the presence of his Creator and Lord on the basis of the information he has. He will write on a piece of paper the name of the person whom he chooses for superior general, and sign it with his name. One hour at most should be given for this. Thereupon all should assemble in their seats. The vicar, together with a secretary to

be chosen for this purpose from among the professed and by another to assist, should arise and attest his wish to admit no one he should not, nor to exclude anyone. He should give to all general absolution from all censures for purposes of the canonical election. After the grace of the Holy Spirit has been invoked, he should go with his companions to a table placed in the center. The three should request their votes from one another; and before handing it over each should pronounce an oath that he is naming the man whom he judges in our Lord most fit for the office. The votes should be kept together in the hands of the secretary. Then they should request each member of the congregation to hand in his vote by himself and in the sight of all, similarly in writing and preceded by the same oath.

The Manner of Reaching a Decision about Matters other than the Election of a General

[711] 1. When the business of the congregation is not the election of a general but other important matters concerning the state of the Society, the enclosure will be unnecessary, although an effort should be made to conclude whatever needs to be treated as speedily as possible. But since the light to perceive what decisions should be taken must come down from the First and Supreme Wisdom, Masses will be said first of all and prayer offered in the place where the congregation is being held as well as throughout the Society, for as long as the congregation continues and the matters it needs to settle are being discussed, in order to obtain grace to decide these matters as may be for the greater glory to God our Lord.

For Prayer, Reflection, and Discussion
What are my reactions and reflections as I ponder these texts in prayer? What reactions and reflections stand out as I reflect on the week? Is the Lord revealing anything to me (us) through my reactions and reflections?

WEEK XVI, DAY 1

These norms stress the Ignatian principles of spiritual governance, a governance whose principal motive is the desire to find God's will. Also Ignatius wants his men to act out of love rather than out of fear.

Preparation for Prayer: see p. 3 of this volume.

What do I desire? That God give me (us) a profound appreciation and love of the Society's way of governance.

On the Governance of the Society
Common Obligations of Superiors
Complementary Norms, Part IX, Chapter 3

349 §1. After the example of Christ, whose place they hold, superiors should exercise their authority in a spirit of service, desiring not to be served but to serve. Government in the Society should always be spiritual, whereby superiors direct our members with discerning love rather than through external laws, conscious before God of personal responsibility and of the obligation to rule their subjects as sons of God and with regard for the human personality. Government should also be strong where it needs to be, open and sincere.

§2. Superiors should devote themselves with a true sense of responsibility to the task of government entrusted to them, not seeking to avoid making plans or decisions by themselves, but with a courageous spirit embarking on great undertakings for the divine service and remaining constant in carrying them out.

350 §1. It is the role of superiors to promote the mission of the Society and observance of the Institute, and to apply it to individuals as circumstances require. In order to do this, they should especially set an example to their subjects as a living norm by which others are constantly drawn to fidelity and generosity in the service of the Lord.

§2. Religious discipline in the Society supposes and produces mature obedient Christian men, superiors as well as members. It is the task of superiors diligently to search for the will of God, also making use of the help of others in regard to the more appropriate means, to decide what is to be done, and to express it definitively in words.

§3. Their greatest duty is to guide all their subjects, especially the younger ones, to ever increasing responsibility and freedom, so that they observe the provisions of our institute not in the spirit of fear but from an intimate personal conviction rooted in faith and charity. Therefore, they should promote religious discipline both paternally and forcefully; they should warn and if necessary correct those who neglect or violate it—even those who are older and respected, and even superiors if they are deficient in their office.

351   Superiors should reckon their governance of our members, both as a community and as individuals, more important than any other tasks.

For Prayer, Reflection, and Discussion

What are my reactions and reflections as I ponder these norms in prayer? Have I experienced these norms being lived out in my life? What has been my experience of superiors in the Society? Is God revealing anything to me (us) through my reactions and reflections?

WEEK XVI, DAY 2

In his Memoriale, *Gonçalves da Câmara, the man to whom Ignatius dictated his autobiography, notes that Ignatius went out of his way to find out what mortified Jesuits wanted to do before missioning them, on the assumption that such men were in touch with God's desires. This principle is enunciated in these norms as well.[10]*

Preparation for Prayer: see p. 3 of this volume.

What do I desire? That God give me (us) a profound appreciation and love of the Society's way of governance.

---

[10] I read this *Memoriale* in French years ago and have not as yet been able to find the reference.

Part IX of the Constitutions and Complementary Norms, on the governance of the Society, *continued*

Common Obligations of Superiors, *continued*
Complementary Norms, Part IX, Chapter 3

352   In the exercise of authority, the gift of discretion or of discerning love is most desirable. To acquire this virtue, the superior should be free from ill-ordered affections and be closely united and familiar with God, so that he will be docile to the will of Christ, which he should seek out with his subjects and authoritatively make manifest to them. He ought to know thoroughly our way of proceeding according to our Institute, and he should command the things that he knows will contribute towards attaining the end proposed by God and the Society, keeping in mind persons, places, times, and other circumstances.

353   The superior should endeavor to make his mind clearly known to his confreres and understood by them; and he should take care that they, according to the nature and importance of the matter and in proportion to their own talents and duties, share more fully in his knowledge and concern both for the personal and community life of our members and for their apostolic labors.

354   §1. Superiors should readily and often ask for and listen to the counsel of their brethren, of a few or of many, or even of all gathered together, according to the importance and nature of the matter, and even by means of spiritual discernment carried out in common (according to no. 151, §2). They should gratefully welcome suggestions that their brothers offer spontaneously, but the duty of superiors themselves to decide and enjoin what ought to be done remains intact.

§2. "Directors of works," of whom nos. 406 and 407 speak, should do the same; they should be altogether alert to the advice and suggestions of their brethren, so as to be helped by them in carrying out their offices.

§3. It is also advantageous to the Society that the superior leave much to the prudence of his confreres, and that he allow them suitable freedom in the Lord to the extent that they have made the spirit of the Society their own, especially if they are men long proven in humility and self-denial. And finally, the universal good itself will sometimes demand that, in the manner of urging what has been commanded, those in charge should also take human frailty into account.

§4. All superiors should work together with the general and all officials with local superiors, in order to encourage implementation of what has been decided, in such a way that all will understand that there is in the Society but a single, identical spirit.

CHAPTER 4

ASSISTANCE GIVEN TO SUPERIORS BY CONSULTORS AND OTHER OFFICIALS

355   §1. In order that they may more easily discover the will of God, all superiors should have their own consultors and should often hear their opinions, ordinarily when all are gathered for a common consultation. They should also use the service of experts in reaching decisions on complex matters.

§2. However, in the Society the consent or advice of consultors is never required in order to act validly, apart from those particular cases specified in the law; but superiors should not act against the unanimous advice of their consultors without the approval of their major superior.

For Prayer, Reflection, and Discussion

What are my reactions and reflections as I ponder these norms in prayer? What has been my experience of superiors in the Society? Have I been consulted about important matters? Has the community been consulted? Is my community moving toward becoming a community that could engage in communal discernment? Is the Lord revealing anything to me (us) through my reactions to these norms?

WEEK XVI, DAY 3

Once again we see Ignatius's prudence and knowledge of human nature. He keeps in the front of his mind the purposes for which the Society has been founded; hence he opts for a lifelong term for the superior general so that the Society will not be distracted from its apostolic purposes by frequent congregations. He also wants to remove the temptation of ambition as far as possible from us Jesuits; hence again a lifelong term. But he foresaw that there might be reasons for a general to resign. Advances of modern medicine have made it imperative to develop further norms for the resignation of a superior general. The Complementary Norms spell out in greater detail how such a resignation might come about. Those interested can look up the details in the Norms themselves.

Preparation for Prayer: see p. 3 of this volume.

What do I desire? That God give me (us) a profound appreciation and love of the Society's way of governance.

On the Governance of the Society, *continued*

The Need of a Superior General and His Lifelong Term of Office

Constitutions, Part IX

[719]   In all well-organized communities or congregations there must be, besides the persons who take care of their particular goals, one or several whose proper duty is to attend to the universal good. So too in this Society, in addition to those who have charge of individual houses or colleges and of the individual provinces where the Society has these houses or colleges, there must be someone with responsibility for the entire body of the Society, a person whose duty is the good government, preservation, and growth of the whole body of the Society. This person is the superior general. While he could be elected in either of two ways, namely, for a fixed period or for his whole life, nevertheless, since experience and practice in government, a knowledge of the individual members *[A]*, and the enjoyment of authority with them *[B]* constitute a great aid in performing this office well, his election will be for life and not for a fixed period. In this way too, the Society, which is commonly occupied with important matters in the divine service, will be less wearied and distracted by general congregations *[C]*.

[720]   *A. Besides the reasons mentioned in this constitution, there are still others for having a general who is elected for life. One is that thoughts and occasions of ambition, which is the pestilence of such offices, will be banished farther than if the general were to be elected at specified intervals.*

Another reason is that it is easier to find one capable person for this charge than many.

Still another reason is the example of the common practice among the more important governmental offices, which are held for life. So it is with the pope and bishops among churchmen and with princes and lords among laymen. With regard to certain disadvantages which could ensue from holding such a charge for life, the remedy will be treated below in Chapter 4 [773–77].

[721]   *B. The superior's authority will be greater if he cannot be changed than if he is elected for one or a few years: greater with the externs because he will be*

better known by all, and greater with the members of the Society for the same reason. On the contrary, the knowledge that he must relinquish his office and be equal or inferior to the others, as also his being new in the office, can lessen his authority.

[722]   *C. It is certain that congregations of the whole Society will occur less frequently if the superior general holds office for life. For the majority of congregations will be convoked to elect him, and other occasions will be few.*

Complementary Norms, Part IX

362   §1. Although the superior general is elected for life and not for any determined time, he may nonetheless in good conscience and by law resign from his office for a grave reason that would render him permanently unequal to the labors of his post.

For Prayer, Reflection, and Discussion

What are my reactions and reflections as I ponder these texts in prayer? What are my reactions to the difficulties attending Father Arrupe's desire to resign and the intervention of Pope John Paul II? Is the Lord revealing anything to me (us) through my reactions and reflections?

WEEK XVI, DAY 4

Many have indicated that Ignatius here all unknowingly drew a portrait of himself. At the least we can see the kind of man he hoped the superior general (and by extension other major superiors) to be. Once again we see the typically Ignatian progression from the interior to the exterior, from the spiritual to the temporal, in the list of qualities of a general superior.

Preparation for Prayer: see p.X 3

What do I desire? That God give me (us) a profound appreciation and love of the Society's way of governance.

On the Governance of the Society, *continued*
The Kind of Person the Superior General Ought to Be
Constitutions, Part IX

[723]   1. In regard to the qualities which are desirable in the superior general *[A]*, the first is that he should be closely united with God our Lord and have familiarity with him in prayer and in all his operations, so that from him, the fountain of all good, he may so much the better obtain for the whole body of the Society a large share of his gifts and graces, as well as great power and effectiveness for all the means to be employed for the help of souls.

[724]   *A. The six qualities treated in this chapter are the most important, the rest being reduced to them. For they comprise the general's perfection in relation to God, together with what perfects his heart, understanding, and execution; and also the corporal and external gifts helpful to him. Moreover, the order of their listing indicates the importance at which they are rated.*

[725]   2. The second quality is that he be a person whose example in all the virtues will be a help to the other members of the Society. Charity towards all his neighbors should particularly shine forth in him, and in a special way toward the members of the Society; likewise a genuine humility which will make him highly beloved of God our Lord and of human beings.

[726]   3. He ought also to be free from all inordinate affections, having them tamed and mortified so that interiorly they will not disturb the judgment of his intellect, and so that exteriorly he will be so composed and, in particular, so circumspect in speaking that none, either members of the Society (who should regard him as a mirror and model) or externs, will observe any thing or word in him that is not edifying.

[727]   4. However, he should know how to mingle the required rectitude and severity with kindness and gentleness in such a way that he neither lets himself be deflected from what he judges to be more pleasing to God our Lord nor fails to have proper sympathy for his sons. Thus even those who are reprimanded or punished will recognize that he proceeds rightly in our Lord and with charity in what he does, even if it is against their liking according to the lower man.

[728]   5. Magnanimity and fortitude of soul are likewise highly necessary for him, so that he may bear the weaknesses of many, initiate great undertakings in the service of God our Lord, and persevere in them with the needed constancy, neither losing courage in the face of the contradictions, even from persons of high rank and power, nor allowing himself to be deflected by their entreaties or threats from what reason and the divine service require. He should be superior to all eventualities, not letting himself be exalted by success or cast down by adversity, and being quite ready to accept death, when neces-

sary, for the good of the Society in the service of Jesus Christ our God and Lord.

[729]   6. The third quality is that he ought to be endowed with great intelligence and judgment, so that he is not lacking in this talent in either speculative or practical matters which may arise. And although learning is highly necessary for one who will have so many learned men in his charge, still more necessary is prudence along with experience in spiritual and interior matters, so that he may be able to discern the various spirits and to give counsel and remedies to so many who will have spiritual necessities. He also needs discretion in exterior matters and a manner of handling such diverse affairs as well as of conversing with such various persons from within and without the Society.

[730]   7. The fourth quality, one highly necessary for the execution of business, is that he should be vigilant and solicitous in undertaking enterprises and vigorous in carrying them through to their completion and perfection, rather than careless and remiss about leaving them begun but unfinished.

[731]   8. The fifth quality concerns the body. As regards health, appearance, and age, account should be taken on the one hand of dignity and authority, and on the other of the physical strength demanded by his charge *[B],* so as to be able therewith to fulfill his office to the glory of God our Lord.

[732]   *B. Thus it seems that he ought to be neither of very advanced age, which is generally unsuited for the labors and cares of such a charge, nor of great youth, which generally is not accompanied by the proper authority and experience.*

[733]   9. The sixth quality regards external things *[C].* Among these preference should be given to those which help more toward edification and the service of God our Lord in such a charge. Such are normally esteem, a good reputation, and whatever else contributes toward authority among those within and without.

[734]   *C. Nobility, wealth which was possessed in the world, honor, and the like are external endowments. Other things being equal, these are worthy of some consideration; but even if they are lacking, there are other things more important which could suffice for election.*

[735]   10. Finally, he ought to be one of those who are most outstanding in every virtue, most deserving in the Society, and known as such for the longest time. If any of the aforementioned qualities should be wanting, he should at least not lack great probity and love for the Society, nor good judgment accompanied by sound learning. In other matters, the aids which he will have (and which will be treated below [789–808]) will be able through God's help and favor to supply for much.

WEEK XVI, DAY 5

In these texts we see the mind of Ignatius with regard to the hierarchy of obedience in the Society. The superior general has all authority in the Society to carry out the Constitutions and the decrees of general congregations. All other authority is delegated. We also see how personal the governance envisioned by Ignatius is supposed to be. The superior general is supposed to know the members as well as he can, at least the men to whom he delegates some of his authority. By the same token the persons who have received some of his authority must in turn know their men.

Preparation for Prayer: see p. 3 of this volume.

What do I desire? That God give me (us) a profound appreciation and love of the Society's way of governance.

On the Governance of the Society, *continued*

The Superior General's Authority over the Society and His Functions

Constitutions, Part IX

[736]   1. It is judged altogether proper for the good government of the Society that the superior general should have complete authority over it, in order to build it up. This authority (from which the general's functions also become manifest) is that described below. [The text then goes on to detail all the areas in which the superior general has authority, including such details as acceptance and dismissal of novices. I include [749] to indicate the flavor of these texts.]

[749]   9. The same general will also have complete authority over missions, in no case contravening those from the Apostolic See, as is stated in Part VII [618]. From those under his obedience, professed or not professed, he may send all he thinks right to any part of the world, for whatever time seems good to him, whether it is definite or indefinite, to exercise any of the means employed by the Society to aid its neighbors. Similarly, he may recall those sent, entirely as he judges to be for the greater glory of God our Lord.

Knowing the talent of those who are under his obedience, he should distribute the offices of preachers, lecturers, confessors, and the like, assigning each subject to the office which he judges in our Lord to be more expedient for the divine service and the good of souls.

[745]   7. Moreover, the provincial and local superiors, rectors, and other commissaries of the general will have such part of this authority as the general communicates to them, and will not need to assemble the members of the colleges collegially for such actions.

[757]   14. Furthermore, he (as has been said in [740, 741]) should personally appoint those whom he judges best fitted for the purpose as the rectors of colleges and universities, and similarly as the local superiors of the houses. He will also appoint the provincials, normally for three years, although he may shorten or lengthen this period when he thinks that this will be conducive to the greater glory of God our Lord *[I]*. He will give to them the power which he judges wise.

[758]   *I. With those who perform their office well and are able to satisfy him in it, nothing is lost by the limitation of three years, since the period can be shortened or lengthened. With those who do not prove apt, something is gained by relieving them without embarrassment when their term is over, unless the general thinks that for the sake of the general good such a person ought to be relieved earlier.*

[759]   15. Likewise, he may revoke, extend, or restrict their authority, and require from them an account of their administration. Furthermore, if he communicates his own authority to the provincial for the appointment of local superiors and rectors, it will remain his part to confirm or remove them.

[764]   19. He should know the consciences, as far as possible, of those whom he has in his charge, especially of the provincial superiors and others to whom he entrusts important responsibilities.

[765]   20. To speak in general, he may command in virtue of obedience all the members in regard to everything conducive to the end which the Society seeks, the perfection and aid of its neighbors for the glory of God. And although he communicates his authority to other superiors or visitors or commissaries, he may approve or revoke the actions they take and in all matters ordain what seems good to him. At all times he should be obeyed and reverenced as one who holds the place of Christ our Lord.

<table>
<tr><td>

For Prayer, Reflection, and Discussion

What are my reactions and reflections as I ponder these texts in prayer? Is the Lord revealing anything to me (us) through my reactions and reflections?

</td></tr>
</table>

WEEK XVI, DAY 6

These norms will serve as an introduction to this day of recapitulation of a week dedicated to the topic of governance in the Society. They take up the role of major superiors and indicate that one of their major roles in these days has to be interprovincial cooperation.

Preparation for Prayer: see p. 3 of this volume.

What do I desire? That God give me (us) a profound appreciation and love of the Society's way of governance.

On the Governance of the Society, *continued*
Superiors of Provinces and Regions (Missions)
Complementary Norms, Part IX, Chapter 2

391   §1. The duty of major superiors is to foster in the provinces or regions entrusted to them religious life, the training of our men, apostolic ministries, and observance of the Constitutions and our Institute; and with the aid of competent assistants, they are to take care of temporal administration, seeking always in all things the greater service of Christ's Church.

§2. Although their power is communicated by the general and is to be exercised under his direction and in subordination to him, this power, as given to them either by common law or the Society's law in virtue of their office, is ordinary power.

§3. The particular and proper duty of major superiors is to visit the houses and works of their province or region. They ought diligently to aid rectors and local superiors in carrying out their own function, showing

aid rectors and local superiors in carrying out their own function, showing demand.

CHAPTER 3

INTERPROVINCE COOPERATION

395 §1. Today many problems are global in nature and therefore require global solutions. Human society itself tends toward a certain unity. Hence, it is appropriate that our Society, which forms one international apostolic body, should live its universal spirit more profoundly, should effectively coordinate its resources and means and strengthen its structures, either those already established or other more flexible ones which render global and regional cooperation easier, so that it may more efficaciously respond to these problems.

§2. According to the genuine spirit of our vocation, that open and complete cooperation which today is more and more a requisite for apostolic action should be promoted among all the Society's members, whatever their province or region, as well as that spirit of union and charity that boldly rejects every brand of particularism and egoism, even of a collective kind, and reaches out readily and generously to the universal good of the Society in the service of God's Church.

397 §1. Major superiors should turn their attention to the needs of the whole Society. They should look on interprovincial and international activities, houses, and works as part of their duty and responsibility and willingly help them according to the measure and proportion worked out by the superior general for each of the individual provinces or regions.

§2. If they judge that because of their proper talents and the movement of grace, some of their subjects would in a special way advance the good of souls in another province, they ought to be prepared, where it seems appropriate, to allow it according to well-ordered charity; moreover, using norms for the choice of ministries in a supernatural spirit, they should not hesitate to discontinue some established works of their own province that seem less useful, in order to undertake a more fruitful or a more needed ministry elsewhere.

WEEK XVII, DAY 1

Part X of the Constitutions summarizes the spirituality of the whole document. It is a recapitulation of "our way to God."

Preparation for Prayer: see p. 3 of this volume.

What do I desire? That God give me (us) a profound appreciation and love of the Society's way of proceeding.

How the Whole Body of the Society Is to Be Preserved and Increased in Its Well-Being

Constitutions, Part X

[812] 1. The Society was not instituted by human means; and it is not through them that it can be preserved and increased, but through the grace of the omnipotent hand of Christ our God and Lord. Therefore in him alone must be placed the hope that he will preserve and carry forward what he deigned to begin for his service and praise and for the aid of souls. In conformity with this hope, the first and most appropriate means will be the prayers and Masses which ought to be offered for this holy intention, and which should be ordered for this purpose every week, month, and year in all places where the Society resides.

[813] 2. For the preservation and growth not only of the body or exterior of the Society but also of its spirit, and for the attainment of the objective it seeks, which is to aid souls to reach their ultimate and supernatural end, the means which unite the human instrument with God and so dispose it that it may be wielded well by his divine hand are more effective than those which equip it in relation to human beings. Such means are, for example, goodness

and virtue, and especially charity, and a pure intention of the divine service, and familiarity with God our Lord in spiritual exercises of devotion, and sincere zeal for souls for the sake of the glory of the one who created and redeemed them and not for any other benefit. Thus it appears that care should be taken in general that all the members of the Society devote themselves to the solid and perfect virtues and to spiritual pursuits, and attach greater importance to them than to learning and other natural and human gifts. For these interior gifts are necessary to make those exterior means efficacious for the end which is being sought.

For Prayer, Reflection, and Discussion

What are my reactions and reflections as I ponder these texts in prayer? Is the Lord revealing anything to me (us) through my reactions and reflections?

WEEK XVII, DAY 2

Once again we see the practical wisdom of Ignatius. The Society must make use of human means once the reliance on God is secured. Here is another tension in Jesuit spirituality that is difficult to hold, a reliance on God and a desire to use all the human talent and means necessary. But the tension is at the heart of Jesuit spirituality. The word translated as "seedbed" (for the professed Society and its coadjutors) is seminario *or* seminarium, *which took on the added meaning of "an institution to train youths."[11] Ignatius, apparently, thought of our schools as places where young men would find their calling to the Society.*

Preparation for Prayer: see p. 3 of this volume.

What do I desire? That God give me (us) a profound appreciation and love of the Society's way of proceeding.

---

[11] See Ganss, *Constitutions of the Society of Jesus,* 333.

How the Whole Body of the Society Is to Be Preserved and Increased in Its Well-Being

Constitutions, Part X

[814]   3. When based upon this foundation, the natural means which equip the human instrument of God our Lord to deal with his fellow human beings will all help toward the preservation and growth of this whole body, provided they are acquired and exercised for the divine service alone; employed, indeed, not so that we may put our confidence in them, but so that we may cooperate with the divine grace according to the arrangement of the sovereign providence of God our Lord. For he desires to be glorified both through the natural means, which he gives as Creator, and through the supernatural means, which he gives as the Author of grace. Therefore the human or acquired means ought to be sought with diligence, especially well-grounded and solid learning, and a method of proposing it to the people by means of sermons, lectures, and the art of dealing and conversing with others.

[815]   4. In a similar manner, it will help greatly to maintain the colleges in good condition and discipline if the superintendency over them is exercised by persons who cannot receive any temporal gain, such as members of the professed Society, which will take care that those who possess the talent for it may receive in the colleges formation in Christian life and learning. For these colleges will be a seedbed for the professed Society and its coadjutors. Furthermore, if universities over which the Society exercises superintendency are added to the colleges, they too will aid toward the same end, as long as the manner of procedure described in Part IV [440–509] is preserved.

For Prayer, Reflection, and Discussion

What are my reactions and reflections as I ponder these texts in prayer? Is the Lord revealing anything to me (us) through my reactions and reflections?

WEEK XVII, DAY 3

Preparation for Prayer: see p. 3 of this volume.

What do I desire? That God give me (us) a profound appreciation and love of the Society's way of proceeding.

Constitutions, Part X

[816]   5. Since poverty is like a bulwark of religious institutes which preserves them in their existence and good order and defends them from many enemies, and since the devil uses corresponding effort to destroy this bulwark in one way or another, it will be highly important for the preservation and growth of this whole body that every appearance of avarice should be banished afar, through the Society's abstention from accepting fixed income, or any possessions, or recompense for preaching, or lecturing, or Masses, or administration of sacraments, or spiritual things, as is stated in Part VI [565], and also through its avoidance of converting the fixed revenue of the colleges to its own utility.

[817]   6. It will also be of the highest importance toward perpetuating the Society's well-being to use great diligence in precluding from it ambition, the mother of all evils in any community or congregation. This will be accomplished by closing the door against seeking, directly or indirectly, any dignity or prelacy within the Society, in such a way that all the professed should promise to God our Lord never to seek one and to expose anyone whom they observe trying to obtain one. . . .

[819]   7. Much aid is given toward perpetuating the well-being of this whole body by what was said in Part I [142–44], Part II [204], and Part V [516–23] about not admitting a mob and persons unsuitable for our Institute, even to probation, and about dismissals during the time of probation when it is found that some persons do not turn out to be suitable. Much less ought those be retained who are addicted to vice or are incorrigible. But even greater strictness should be shown in admitting persons among the approved scholastics [approved brothers are included among the scholastics; see *CN* no. 6, §1, 2°] and formed coadjutors, and strictness far greater still in regard to admission to profession. This profession should be made only by persons who are select in spirit and learning, and who after prolonged and extensive activity have become well known through various trials of virtue and abnegation, with edification and satisfaction to all. This is done so that, even though numbers grow, the spirit may not be diminished or weakened, with those incorporated into the Society being such as has been described.

WEEK XVII, DAY 4

Preparation for Prayer: see p. 3 of this volume.

What do I desire? That God give me (us) a profound appreciation and love of the Society's way of proceeding.

Constitutions, Part X

[820] 8. Since the well-being or illness of the head has its consequences in the whole body, it is supremely important that the election of the superior general be carried out as directed in Part IX [723–35]. Next in importance is the choice of the lower superiors in the provinces, colleges, and houses of the Society. For in a general way, the subjects will be what these superiors are.

It is also highly important that, in addition to that choice, the individual superiors should have much authority over the subjects, and the general over the individual superiors; and, on the other hand, that the Society have much authority in regard to the general, as is explained in Part IX [736, 757, 759, 766–88]. This arrangement is made so that all may have full power for good and that, if they do poorly, they may be fully in subjection.

It is similarly important that the superiors have suitable helpers, as was said in the same part [798–810], for the good order and execution of the affairs pertaining to their office.

[821] 9. Whatever helps toward the union of the members of this Society among themselves and with their head will also help much toward preserving the well-being of the Society. This is especially the case with the bond of wills, which is the mutual charity and love they have for one another. This bond is strengthened by their getting information and news from one another and having much intercommunication, by their following one same doctrine, and by

their being uniform in everything as far as possible, and above all by the bond of obedience, which unites the individuals with their superiors, and the local superiors among themselves and with the provincials, and both the local superiors and provincials with the general, in such a way that the subordination of some to others is diligently preserved.

For Prayer, Reflection, and Discussion

What are my reactions and reflections as I ponder these texts in prayer? Is the Lord revealing anything to me (us) through my reactions and reflections?

WEEK XVII, DAY 5

Preparation for Prayer: see p. 3 of this volume.

What do I desire? That God give me (us) a profound appreciation and love of the Society's way of proceeding.

Constitutions, Part X

[822]   10. Moderation in spiritual and bodily labors and the middle tenor of the Constitutions, which do not lean toward an extreme of rigor or toward excessive laxity (and thus they can be better observed), will help this whole body to persevere and maintain itself in its well-being.

[823]   11. Toward the same purpose it is helpful in general to strive to retain the goodwill and charity of all, even of those outside the Society, and especially of those whose favorable or unfavorable attitude toward it is of great importance for opening or closing the gate leading to the service of God and the good of souls *[B]*. It is also helpful that in the Society there should neither be partiality to one side or another among Christian princes or rulers nor should any be perceived; in its stead there should be a universal love which embraces in our Lord all parties (even though they are adversaries to one another).

[824]   *B. We must chiefly retain the benevolence of the Apostolic See, which the Society must especially serve; and then that of the temporal rulers and noble and powerful persons whose favor or disfavor does much toward opening or closing the gate to the service of God and the good of souls. Similarly, when an unfavorable attitude is noticed in some persons, especially in persons of importance, prayer ought to be offered for them and the suitable means should be employed to bring them to friendship, or at least to keep them from being hostile. This is done, not because contradiction and ill-treatment are feared, but so that God our Lord may be more served and glorified in all things through the benevolence of all these persons.*

[825]   12. Help will also be found in a discreet and moderate use of the favors granted by the Apostolic See, by seeking with all sincerity nothing else than the aid of souls. For through this God our Lord will carry forward what he has begun; and the fragrance [2 Cor. 2:15] arising from the genuineness of the good works will increase the benevolent desire of others to avail themselves of the Society's aid and to help the Society for the end which it seeks, the glory and service of his Divine Majesty.

[826]   13. It will also be helpful that attention should be devoted to the preservation of the health of the individual members *[C]*, as was stated in Part III [292–306]; and finally, that all should apply themselves to the observance of the Constitutions. For this purpose they must know them, at least those which pertain to each one. Therefore each one should read or hear them every month.

[827]   *C. For this purpose it is expedient that attention should be given to having the houses and colleges in healthy locations with pure air and not in those characterized by the opposite.*

A.M.D.G.

For Prayer, Reflection, and Discussion

What are my reactions and reflections as I ponder these texts in prayer? Is the Lord revealing anything to me (us) through my reactions and reflections?

WEEK XVII, DAY 6

We come to the end of this prayerful reflection on "our way to God." These norms from our latest congregations give us a chance to reflect on the past week in which we have contemplated Part X of the Constitutions and, during the past seventeen weeks of this prayerful time of reflection, reflected on our way of proceeding. May the Lord bring to completion the good work which he has begun in us.

Preparation for Prayer: see p. 3 of this volume.

What do I desire? That God give me (us) a profound appreciation and love of the Society's way of proceeding.

Complementary Norms, Part X
The Preservation and Increase of the Society

410   §1. As a sign of gratitude and devotion to the Sacred Heart of Jesus, let that feast be solemnly celebrated; and on that day is to be renewed the consecration by which the Society on January 1, 1872, dedicated and consecrated itself totally and perpetually.

§2. The consecration to the Immaculate Heart of the Blessed Virgin Mary is to be renewed each year on the feast of the Immaculate Heart.

411   The sense of belonging and responsibility that each individual one of Ours has toward the whole Society should be manifested in a knowledge of our spirituality, our history, our saints, our apostolic labors, and our men, especially of those who are suffering difficulties for the sake of Christ; it is to be manifested as well by maintaining Ignatian mobility and flexibility with a view to helping any region of the Society whatsoever.

412   §1. All our members should have at heart a shared concern for attracting new members to the Society, especially by prayer and the example of their lives as individuals and in community. ·

§2. Therefore, we must do everything possible actively to present the Society in such a way that those whom God calls will know and appreciate who and what we are and what is our distinctive way of proceeding in the following of Christ.

§3. We must also promote vocations as widely as possible, in order to reflect the culture and experience of those we seek to serve, including minority cultures, immigrants, and indigenous people.

413   The Society should always show itself bound to its benefactors in charity and gratitude. Superiors should ensure that prayers are offered for them and other appropriate signs of our gratitude are shown them.

414   "In the perfect observance of all the Constitutions and in the particular fulfillment of our Institute," our formed members should excel, setting a good example and spreading the good odor of Christ, keeping before their eyes the serious obligation they have of giving edification especially to our younger members.

415   All by earnest reading and meditation (in particular, at the time of the annual Spiritual Exercises, renewal of vows, monthly recollection, beginning of the year, and so forth) should strive ever to know, esteem, and love better our Constitutions and the special nature of our Institute, which are to be faithfully observed, and which for each and all of us are the one, true, and safe way that surely leads to the perfection to which our Lord calls and invites all sons of the Society.

§2. Major superiors, especially at the time of the annual visitation, should see that this is faithfully observed.

416   Finally, those means that are proposed by our holy father Saint Ignatius in Part X of the Constitutions "for the preservation and development not only of the body or exterior of the Society but also of its spirit, and for the attainment of the objective it seeks, which is to aid souls to reach their ultimate and supernatural end," are to be observed eagerly and diligently by all, with a truly personal sense of responsibility for its increase and development, for the praise and service of our God and Lord Jesus Christ, and the help of souls.

L. D. S.

For Prayer, Reflection, and Discussion

What are my reactions and reflections as I ponder these texts in prayer? Is the Lord revealing anything to me (us) through my reactions and reflections?

Contemplation to Obtain Love

It might be appropriate here to recall the final contemplation of the Spiritual Exercises. Like that contemplation for the Exercises, Part X of the Constitutions is the capstone of Ignatius's mystical work. The text of the Contemplation is presented here, at the end of these reflections.

Note. Two preliminary observations should be made.

First. Love ought to manifest itself more by deeds than by words.

Second. Love consists in a mutual communication between the two persons. That is, the one who loves gives and communicates to the beloved what he or she has, or a part of what one has or can have; and the beloved in return does the same to the lover. Thus, if the one has knowledge, one gives it to the other who does not; and similarly in regard to honors or riches. Each shares with the other. (no. 230–31)

With the first observation Ignatius does not deprecate the expression of one's love for another; rather, he rightly acknowledges that words alone do not prove love. The second observation contains a mind-boggling idea when applied to God; namely, that God wants mutuality, that God wants something from each of us human beings. What can we give to God? What does God need? If God is God, then God needs nothing, lacks nothing. However, God freely decides to want something when God creates persons called to enter into the community life of the Trinity. In order to be the God God wants to be for us, we must respond to the call to intimate union.

The First Point. I will call back into my memory the gifts I have received—my creation, redemption, and other gifts particular to myself. I will ponder with deep affection how much God our Lord has done for me, and how much he has given me of what he possesses, and consequently how he, the same Lord, desires to give me even his very self, in accordance with his divine design.

Then I will reflect on myself, and consider what I on my part ought in all reason and justice to offer and give to the Divine Majesty, namely, all my possessions, and myself along with them. I will speak as one making an offering with deep affection, and say:

"Take, Lord, and receive all my liberty, my memory, my understanding, and all my will—all that I have and possess. You, Lord, have given all that to me. I now give it back to you, O Lord. All of it is yours. Dispose of it according to your will. Give me love of yourself along with your grace, for that is enough for me." (no. 234)

The Second Point. I will consider how God dwells in creatures; in the elements, giving them existence; in the plants, giving them life; in the animals, giving them sensation; in human beings, giving them intelligence; and finally, how in this way he dwells also in myself, giving me existence, life, sensation, and intelligence; and even further, making me his temple, since I am created as a likeness and image of the Divine Majesty. Then once again I will reflect on myself, in the manner described in the first point, or in any other way I feel to be better. This same procedure will be used in each of the following points. (no. 235)

The Third Point. I will consider how God labors and works for me in all the creatures on the face of the earth; that is, he acts in the manner of one who is laboring. For example, he is working in the heavens, elements, plants, fruits, cattle, and all the rest—giving them their existence, conserving them, concurring with their vegetative and sensitive activities, and so forth. Then I will reflect on myself. (no. 236)

The Fourth Point. I will consider how all good things and gifts descend from above; for example, my limited power from the Supreme and Infinite Power above; and so of justice, goodness, piety, mercy, and so forth—just as the rays come down from the sun, or the rains from their source. Then I will finish by reflecting on myself, as has been explained. I will conclude with a colloquy and an Our Father. (no. 237)